THE POWER OF ECCLESIASTICAL THINKING

"Life's Simplicity"

By: Anita M. Hopes

Table of Contents

ACKNOWLEDGEMENTS

Assuredly, I cannot take credit for writing this book. In all honesty, as I've penned the words, I have been extremely aware of the awesome presence of God. Almost instantly I sensed his overwhelming desire and longing to communicate truths to his creation. I am honored and grateful for the privilege to be His mouthpiece.

May you ever be encouraged and inspired to live this abundant life to its fullest in Christ and find what you're looking for as you realize your completeness in God through the Lord Jesus Christ

.

Knowing that we are subsequently woven together in this life, one with another, I must express my great appreciation and love for everyone whose life has intertwined with mine. You are an incredible blessing! "Thank you, God for surrounding me with great people, residing on earth and in heaven."

I'd like to thank my three beautiful children whom God has so tremendously used to make me who I am. Your gifting, personalities and love over the years has served to mold my character. Crystal, your kindness and genuine love has meant so much to me. Thanks for allowing me an entrance into your life.. It is an honor and pleasure being your stepmom.

Albert, you are such a jewel. God has graced you with a gift for laughter and great joy. It's effortless and spontaneous and brings healing to many. You have such an incredible understanding of his grace and mercy, and have taught me the practicality of God and to rest in Him.

Sherina, you are such a unique woman. Your love of God, generosity and giving heart permeates your being and shines through to others. I love to sit and listen to your worship. When you sing, it's like the angels are singing around His throne. The world is waiting on your CD.

Thank you all for hanging in there with me as I grew into the woman God created." I love you beyond words. I am so proud of each of you for being who you are!

Mom, of course you not only supplied the birth canal through which I entered this world, but also have been a one of a kind mother and a great friend and prayer partner. It is the godly foundational teachings that you instilled in me from birth that have contributed to forming my character and attributed to my great love for God and all that He is.

When I think of where I would be without my siblings, Donald, Stanley, Anthony, and Malinda, I would not be writing this book. Each of you has given so much of yourself to me, that I am convinced part of me is derived from you. If I were given the opportunity to choose my brothers and sister again, I'd choose you Donald for his strength and wisdom; Stanley for his laughter and teasing; Anthony for his love and joy; and Malinda, for her courage, wisdom, compassion and class. Reanee', you entered our family through marriage, it's like Mom birthed you. Your love and great smile are amazing!

Thank you, Ryan for being one of my biggest fans. Your encouragement means so much to me. That's why I give a "shout" out to you today!

And what great joy has been added to my life by the entrance of my wonderful grandchildren; I love you all. Taylor, your smile is gorgeous; Shayla, your joy is infectious and overflowing; Tiffany, you are unique, and Amaris, your worship is outstanding. Thank you, my blessings, for expanding my territory!

I extend many blessings to my sons-in-law, Brian and Freeman. Brian, what a delight and joy it is to have you in our family. Freeman, as a new comer we welcome you!

Our hearts are everlasting knitted by love in the heart of an Eternal God. Your accomplishments are my accomplishments, your victories, my victories and your joy is my joy! "Thanks family."

Finally, I take this moment to acknowledge and thank all the pastors and friends who have contributed their time and ministry gifts to my life. Your guidance, spiritual insight, love and friendship are appreciated more than I could ever express. Pastors, you've left an indelible mark on me. May our Father God remember all your acts of love and grant your heart's desires.

Bishop Robert E. Joyce, you've taught me to be confident in Christ and the prophetic gift he has placed in me, and enabled me to launch out into the deep. Pastor Marvin L. Winans, through instruction and demonstration I have learned the depth of a shepard's love for his sheep, and the importance of excellence in all I do. Pastor Ralph Siegel, you have taught me how to care for others, and to raise up leaders. Dr. Gary V. Whetstone, you have grounded me in righteous and grace, and given me a surpassing understanding of victory in spiritual warfare. I am also eternally grateful to Rev. C. Grant Hammond, my first Bible teacher and pastor, now residing in heaven, for igniting in me a fire and passion for God!

Also, "Thank you, God for my most precious prayer partner and friend, Karen." For the many late hours you have poured out before the Father for my family, Karen, and your selfless love, may God reward you and grant you much sleep.

INTRODUCTION

As I begin to write this book on, "The Power of Ecclesiastical Thinking," I find an astronomical amount of resistance. Although my pen and mind are ready, fatigue strikes me, fear screams loudly to my inner man, and doubt invades the privacy of my mind. I know without a shadow of a doubt, that I am to write this, and so write it I shall.

Let's begin by defining the term "Ecclesiastes," a humongous word that sometimes deters readers from delving into this seemingly secretive book. However, if I have learned anything, I've learned "simplicity."

Ecclesiastes in Hebrew is "koheleth" and in English is interpreted, "preacher:" We know a preacher to be one to whom we normally attribute wisdom, someone who has the ability or gifting to expound on the Word of God (to herald or proclaim a message). How fitting a title, since this book gives great insight and wisdom on understanding life and successfully walking through its portals.

Have you ever wished that there was a book or some writings somewhere that would help you live successfully in this life? You want just a little direction, something to let you know what your next step is. You say to yourself, "I'm here on this earth, but why? I don't have a clue! What am I supposed to be doing and am I doing the right thing? Who knows? It's like you've been placed here, but what's next? What should I do? Why do I do what I do; and is there a better way? If so, how do I find it?"

Come with me into the "Land of Answers" as we unravel the pages of this marvelous book and discover hidden jewels strategically deposited by God for the purpose of guiding us to our fulfilled destinies. Having said that, let's begin at the beginning.

Since King Solomon was the wisest man who ever lived; he was loaded with great wisdom! Can you imagine the thoughts of his mind? He searched out the reason for everything, thinking all the time, reasoning day and night on the meaning of everything and how to apply what he had learned. Remember that wisdom is the practical application of knowledge!

In his search of the true meaning of folly, he decided to find a way to drink wine and hold onto his understanding, endeavoring not to allow it to be affected by the wine! He built great works, many houses, vineyards filled with various fruit trees, elaborate pools, and his houses were filled with the best of the best! He hired servants to tend to all he had. Solomon's wealth was astronomical! He accumulated more than anyone who had ever lived! He had this entire kingdom plus, God never removed his wisdom from him.

At the culmination of his life, he concluded that all this was vanity, as trying to catch the wind -- it's of no profit! After much examination, it became quite evident that this is all madness, foolishness, and great folly. It's plain silly! Human wisdom apart from God never makes sense. And yet, even human wisdom far exceeds the folly of foolishness; these two are as far apart as night and day. The day or light is far better than the dark.

Chapter One

<u>NOTHING NEW</u>

Ever wonder if you're making a good choice for your life? What will your next decision hold for you and those closest to you?

I'm sure King Solomon asked himself these same questions. After all, he was the man who God anointed with great wisdom, the man who tried so many different things to find out the true meaning of life. In the end, he writes that all is vanity (emptiness or a chasing after the wind). Wow! I guess knowing this at the onslaught of life makes it easier not to get attached to things, positions, accomplishments, etc…, because all is temporal or vanity. It's like the grass that grows today and tomorrow is cut down.

The writer begins by asking us a very poignant question. **"What profit hath a man of all his labor which he taketh under the sun?"** What is the profit of your life's labor?

At this point you may reference your great wealth, your seemingly notable accolades, and your fond remembrances of past accomplishments, all of which are due notable applause; however, when life for you is over, as you know it on earth, what profit do you have? What tangible thing can be taken with you?

The sun labors, the moon labors, (rising and setting daily), the wind labors, the rivers labor as they blow into the sea, and man labors. How different is man from these?

Knowing that every course of life has been and shall be again, what manner of man ought you to be in your everyday living? Nothing is new under the sun! Our lives are but a vapor, like a puff of smoke that arises for a short time and is then blown away. Nothing is new! Even new life is old, meaning that from the moment we are born, we begin counting our days and years. We celebrate our birth date, which continually reminds us of the aging process.

King Solomon is asking us to think about life and what is really important in it. Nothing is new, and what has been shall be again! What is, has already been before. Think about it, once you are gone from this life in years to come there may be virtually no remembrance of you, or the great pains you exerted in accomplishing your goals. Neither will these be credence for the sleepless nights you spent in worrying over what might be or what is. What will you say then, after considering all of this?

<u>Food For Thought</u>

1. **Can you think of times you worried or concerned over something that never came to pass?**

2. **How many hours and days were lost from your life?**

3. How could you have been more productive with your time?

4. What would have been a better choice for you to do about the situation instead of worrying?

5. How can you eliminate worry and stress from your life?

6. How can removing stress and worry from your life help those you are in a direct relationship with?

- Take time to reflect on the beauty that God has created. Notice how life continues without your help, the birds fly, the rain falls, the sun rises, and the seasons remain.

- Perhaps you could journal your communication with God, your prayers and the answers. Always remember that God wants the best for you. He is always on your side. He will never let you down, even when others do. Focusing on how big God is will allow you to see how small your situations are.

- Keep in mind that God knew your end before the beginning and that He will work everything for good that concerns you.

Chapter Two

LET'S GO!

Are you anxious and concerned about the things of this life? Do you sometimes wonder what shall become of it all? Take heart! God says that it's all in His hands. After all, there is someone who has already mapped out the times and seasons.

Solomon tells us in chapter 2 of Ecclesiastes, that everything has an appointed time and season. No one lives forever. The question is, "What will you do with the life you are given? We shall someday die and leave our works to someone else. Will he be foolish or wise? We do not know. So he says to enjoy this life, (eat, drink, and enjoy) knowing this, that **God will give to him that is good in his sight, wisdom, knowledge, and joy.** He will take from the sinner and give to the good man. In light of this, strive to make each day the best day of your life!

In chapter 2 of Ecclesiastes, the writer sought to explore the depths of foolishness and to report his findings, thereby alleviating us from the despairs of this journey. In an attempt to fully understand foolishness and the benefits or detriments thereof, he spared nothing and denied himself no pleasure. At the conclusion of his exploration, he summarizes that it was all vanity, (empty, and futile). It brought no lasting results! He found laughter (in its carnal state) to be mad and pleasure to be without accomplishment. In other words, apart from God none of this is satisfying.

The light offers a clear path to walk in, while the dark hides many obstacles and stumbling blocks. "Thy word, O Lord, is a lamp unto my feet and a light unto my pathway." For the wise man, his eyes are in his head (his thinking), and he sees clearly his next step(s), but the foolish man has no clarity of sight. For instance, the wise man gets God's thoughts in an area, develops a plan of action and considers every intricate detail. He depends upon the Holy Spirit's anointing to help him work the plan and follow through. A fool on the other hand, has no plan and is void of any understanding. – Even his continual thoughts are foolish, or of "no value." He walks in darkness. He may even have faith but without works, (an activated plan), it is dead, "of no value."

So, you would say that it is better to be a man of great wisdom than a fool, void of understanding! I would be inclined to agree with you, except for the fact that even a wise man, apart from God, walks in error. Both the wise man and the fool die, leaving all.

Let me interject a ray of hope here! The man, who knows God, and has accepted Jesus Christ (His Son) as his Lord and Savior, has been washed in the shed Blood of Christ and will enter into eternal glory in God's presence when he dies. In II Cor. 5:8 it states, "rather to be absent from the body (in death), is to be present with the Lord." Hallelujah!

Even so, as far as this earth's stay is concerned, death is inevitable for all and all accumulated wealth, fame, family and friends must be left behind. It is a walk that each man must take alone. We leave everything to another who remains on the earth and who knows if he will be a man of wisdom or a fool!

So, ask yourself, "Why are you doing what you are doing?" Has God ordained it? God gives to the good man, wisdom, knowledge, and joy. Wisdom is the practical application of knowledge. You can possess much knowledge, but without the knowing or understanding of how to make it work, it is empty. For example, I may desire to take a trip to some distant land and through my research I find out about all its wonderful attractions, including gorgeous beaches with pure white sand and breath taking sunsets, or perhaps mountain slopes with sunrays that kiss the white sparkling snow. It may have a thriving economy and be filled with breath-taking, five-star hotels, complete with the ambiance for a king, (scenic view, luxurious dining areas, even diamond shaped pools), and all the amenities imaginable, but unless I possess the wisdom to prepare properly for the trip, I will not be going anywhere!

In this particular scenario, wisdom would tell me to count the cost, consider how man vacation days I can reasonably devote to this trip, map out all the intricate details of my stay, make the reservations, plan how I'll get to and from the airport, and so on. Wisdom truly is the practical application of knowledge! Without wisdom, knowledge is void of understanding, similar to how faith without works is dead or unproductive.

Spiritually, you may have great faith so as to move huge mountains, but unless you do the necessary work to accompany your faith, the mountains will remain and you will be frustrated or disillusioned with God.

There was a time in my life when I heard the Lord instruct me to hold a Women's Conference. I planned it to the "t", assigning a staff to work with me, booked the hotel, and everything except holding the conference! The conference was dead because I didn't complete the works by sending out fliers and notices. How was anyone to know? Nobody really knew about it and nobody received what God had ordained. I felt really bad and lost my joy. Wisdom in Hebrew is "chokmah", skillful wisdom, and knowledge is know or aware. Webster defines joy as great pleasure, happiness, delight, or to rejoice and in the Hebrew language it is "simchah", meaning blithesomeness or glee, gladness, mirth, pleasure, and rejoice. Had I continued walking in faith, I would have experienced this gladness and joy. So when you have the knowledge coupled with the wisdom, practical application, then you can have joy. Why? Your plans have now advanced from just a thought or series of thoughts to a manifestation of the desires!

I have found many times in the Body of Christ that there is what is termed "faith" that produces deadness. Why? There is no wisdom applied, just belief. But remember that just as faith without works is dead (or fruitless) so also knowledge without wisdom is unproductive and useless. However, it is God who gives to the man who pleases Him (good in His sight) wisdom and knowledge and joy! So this must come from God!

Remember that there is a difference between "faith" and "presumption". God will give you specific wisdom on an area and expect you to act on it. However, presumption is presuming or supposing that you are to do something without really knowing for sure. You presume you are to do something, and then after doing it, you find that it is fruitless.

This is where frustration sets in and then sometimes you get upset with God and feel that He has let you down, when in actuality, you acted on presumption and not faith.

I find a good way to know if its faith or presumption is this: If I'm led by the Holy Spirit to follow a certain path, then it's faith. But, if I'm led by my own thoughts or desires, then normally it's presumption. For instance, I once wanted to go to a large conference where I felt I'd be ministered to and receive exactly what I needed for the next phase in ministry. Well, I did everything in the natural to get there, but it didn't happen. I even spent money on a non-refundable registration. Financially, I didn't have the extra money during that time to spend on a conference. The finances were allotted for other things. Now, was God leading me there? No, I was. I presumed that He wanted me there, and that miraculously, He would send the finances. But, if I had listened to the still small voice of the Holy Spirit within my spirit, I would not have acted presumptuously. (Wisdom is the practical application of knowledge.)

The following year, however, it happened! I went to the conference. The oddest thing is that it was not accomplished by my own choosing. In fact, I desired to stay at home and give my plane ticket, hotel accommodations, and registration to someone else. The Holy Spirit led me there for His purpose, and I was so blessed. Has that ever happened to you? How did you handle the situation? Let me encourage you to allow God to lead you, and if you ever miss it, don't allow condemnation or guilt to take up residence in your mind. Check it at the door!

The conclusion of chapter two says that to the sinner God gives the work or toil (labor) of gathering and heaping up that he may give to the one that pleases God. The scripture says in Proverbs 13:22, "The wealth of the wicked is laid up for the righteous."
God has the wicked man toiling long tireless hours for the righteous man's benefit. This is something that the human mind cannot figure out; it's like trying to catch the wind. No one can catch the wind and so likewise, no one can figure this out. It is God's will and his way of doing things.

God promised to bless the work of the righteous man's hands and so when he puts his hands to the work, God blesses it and causes him to prosper. The wealth is then transferred to his house. But to the sinner, God gives the labor of gathering up endlessly to give to the righteous ones who please him. How does a man please God? Well, the word of God says in Hebrews 11:6 that without faith it is impossible to please God. So we must operate in faith. Consider also Deut. 28:1-14 which lists all the blessings that shall come upon us and overtake us. This just means that we do what's right in his sight, walking in His uprightness and holiness.

- Blessed in the city and blessed in the field.

- Fruit of your body is blessed, and fruit of your ground and beasts, the increase of your cattle and the increase of your flock (all you have).

- Blessed shall be your basket and kneading trough (work and provision).

- Blessed when you come in and when you go out (at all times).

- Your enemies who come against you are defeated. They shall come against you one way and flee seven ways (in a hurry!).

- The Lord commands the Blessing upon you in your storehouse and in all you undertake (Blessed in your bank account and all you do).

- Blessed in the land which the Lord your God <u>gives</u> you (where you live).

- Established as a people holy to Himself, (God will settle and establish you.)

- All the people of the earth shall see that you are called by His name and they shall be afraid of you. (They'll see that God is with you, establishing and prospering you and they shall be afraid to go against you!)

- The Lord shall give you a surplus of prosperity through the fruit of your body, your livestock and your ground in the land He gives you. (Surplus promised and given)

Food For Thought

1. **Reflect on the things you've been occupied with this week, whether occupied in your mind or the actual doing of the task. Have you had any concerns or worries, things you felt were just a little too hard for God? If so, why? 1 Peter 5:7 reminds us to, "Cast all your cares upon the Lord, for He cares for you." Cast means to toss as a football.**

2. **List the areas you lack confidence in. These are areas you just can't let go of, and you're not confident that God will do it for you. Many times when we find these concerns constantly coming into our minds, it identifies a "lack of trust". God reassures us of his presence and help.**

Proverbs 3:5 "Trust (rely on, and depend on, put total confidence) in the Lord with all your heart, and lean (in your mind) not unto your own understanding. In all your ways acknowledge Him (God) and He shall direct your path." Do you need more wisdom in order to live a more content and successful life? Take a moment and write down these areas, then ask God for wisdom. Ask Him to bring godly people into your life who can instruct you in each area.

James 1:5 says, "If any of you lack wisdom, let him ask of God, that giveth to all men liberally and upbraideth not; and it shall be given him. Proverbs 11:14 says, "Where no counsel is, the people fall; but in the multitude of counselors there is safety."

3. Every so often I like to check my joy thermometer. Have you checked yours lately? In Ecclesiastes chapter 2, we learned that when we're doing what God has instructed, and walking in wisdom, joy is manifested.

Remember, God gives to the man that is good in His sight, wisdom, knowledge, and joy! "The joy of the Lord is your strength." (Neh. 8:10)

Chapter Three

The Master Plan

God has so designed everything with such precise detail, even intricately fashioning each man and his surroundings so minutely that nothing is just "happenstance." Clearly no event in time past, time present, or future is by any will of man. **The Master has designed a plan that is infallible!**

Think of the times when your path has crossed that of another individual who was exactly the person you needed to interact with at that particular moment in your life. The world coins this as a "coincidence," but I know it to be God's divine appointments. You may say that this only applies to the righteous, but I would say, "No, no, he rains upon the just as well as the unjust, for his mercy endures forever.

There are seasons in God, and everything has a season to begin, endure, and end. Everything has a time and a purpose. What is a season? The Hebrew meaning is "an appointed occasion." Appointed by whom and for what purpose? Appointed by God for the purpose he preordained or pre-ordered before you ever arrived on the scene! Your life has been pre-ordered by God and filled with divine connections and purpose.

This makes me think of me ordering takeout food at a restaurant. I call ahead and place my order exactly how I want it, I do not leave out one detail. I'd order a succulent filet mignon steak well done, smothered with sautéed onions and mushrooms, homemade whipped potatoes with butter, and fresh onion marinated stir-fried green beans. And the grand finale would be a large slice of rich carrot cake and a cup of creamy French vanilla decaffeinated coffee. Mmmm, as I'm writing this, my mouth is watering as my mind pictures this awesome meal. Delicious!

Now when I arrive at the restaurant to pick it up, I expect it to be exactly as I ordered it. Why do I say this? I took the time to pre-send my order to the cook. I wouldn't expect to get there and be handed a hamburger, fries, and a soft drink. No, rather I expect to receive exactly what I ordered!

So it is with God. He has pre-ordered our lives here on earth with exact details of times and circumstances. Everything has a season and a time. Everything has a time to begin and a time to end. So, remember, when you go through a season of great joy or a season of hardship, it is only "a season;" it's an appointed time or occasion with a beginning, middle, and ending.

God told the great prophet Jeremiah that before he was born, He knew him, (He knew him intimately) and before he came forth out of his mother's womb, He sanctified him (set him apart), and called him to be a prophet to the nations. In other words, everything was already planned!

Let me elaborate on the times and seasons preplanned and prepared for us before we are born. I love this particular passage in the Bible. In I Samuel chapters 9 and 10, we learn of an event in a young man named Saul's life. His father, Kish's donkeys were lost, so Kish ordered his son to take a "**certain**" servant with him and go find them. The Bible says that they journeyed far and could not find them. They passed through the hill country of Ephraim and the land of Shalishah, then through Shaalim and then Benjamin. Finally they came to Zuph, but by this time Saul began to get worried about his father. He knew that his father would be upset and now no longer be concerned about the donkeys but worrying about him. So he said to this "**certain**" servant, "Let's return."

Now, had he gone alone, he would have automatically returned at this point; however, this **particular** servant knew this territory and also that a prophet of God dwelt here to whom God revealed things. He suggested they go see the prophet first before turning back. This would have been wonderful, except Saul didn't have any money and it was customary to always bring a gift to the prophet. Other servants may not have had any money, but this "**certain**" one did; he had "a" coin to give as an offering!

As they climbed the hill toward the city, they "**happened**" to meet young ladies on their way to draw water from the well, and inquired if they knew where the prophet lived. They "**happened**" to know that he had just come this **particular** day and time to the city to bless the sacrifice the people were offering. The young ladies told Saul and his servant "**exactly**" where to find the prophet, Samuel before he went up to the sacrifice. Could this be a "coincidence?"

Just as they arrived at their destination, they met a man of whom they inquired if he knew where the prophet resided, and the man "**happened**" to be Samuel, the prophet. Could this be a divine appointment?

What neither of these two wearied travelers knew was that God had already spoken to the prophet the day before (previously), that the next day at a **particular** time he would send a man from the land of Benjamin for him to anoint as leader over Israel. God said that this man would save them out of the hands of the Philistines, for God had looked upon the distress of his people and heard their cries unto him.

As the men approached Samuel, God spoke to him and pointed out Saul as the Benjamite man he was sending saying, "This is the man of whom I told you. He shall have authority over my people." Samuel invited Saul to be his guest at the sacrificial meal he was offering to God. At the beginning of the meal, Samuel told the cook to bring out the "choice" piece of meat he was saving. When the cook returned with this portion, Samuel ordered it be given to Saul, (the man he was honoring). What's even more important is that this piece was reserved for the priest. I'm sure that by this time Saul was floored, he didn't know what to make of all of this? Why was he, a little Benjamite young man, the least of the tribes of Israel, being honored? He had done nothing to warrant this!

Now comes the best part. Samuel said, "See what was **reserved** for you." This honor had been reserved (preordered) for him by God. He said, "Eat, for until the hour

appointed (season) it was kept for you…" God has some appointed blessings that have been kept for you and will be released in a pre-determined season and time in your life. Just assuredly as he had this for Saul, he has them for you. **Saul had to endure a season of uncertainty or trial before coming into his season of honor and blessings, and so do we.** There is always a beginning and an end to every season.

Sometimes it seems that life is mundane. We continue day and night to do "routine things." We are always waiting to do the "big thing," not realizing that the routine things over a period of time turn into the "big thing." Saul had to be content with taking care of his father's business no matter how routine or unimportant it seemed. He also, had to do it with a smile and a willing heart. What seemed to Saul as a routine search for the donkeys turned out to be a divine appointment by God for **promotion**.

If we continue reading in the Book of 1 Samuel, we'll see that Samuel anointed Saul to be king over Israel, told him that the donkeys had been found, that now his father is worrying about him, and all the events that would await him on this journey back home. Everything the prophet told him came to pass.

This journey was set up by God to get Saul to the Prophet Samuel so he could speak God's word over him. How beautifully this expresses the extent God will go to in order to get His blessings to us.

Ecclesiastes says that to everything there is a season, and a time under heaven (or here on earth). There's a time to be born and a time to die (as the grass that springs up today and withers and dies, so are the days of man). There's a time to plant and a time to pluck up (sowing and reaping), a time to kill and a time to heal.

There were times when certain things in my life had to be killed; in other words, I went through some rough and painful times in order to kill some things in me that were not like God, even attitudes and actions that were engrained in my character. Yet, there are also times when God has brought a lasting healing to my wounded emotions. Allow God to walk you through your seasons and tests, remember, **"Don't abort."** It's necessary to follow it all the way through in order to come into your blessing, and once you passed the test in an area, you need not go through it again.

There is also a time to break down or tear down for the purpose of building up. In life many times it seems that we don't have answers for the challenges we face, but know that it could be a part of the tearing down for the purpose of building up. I like to think of the remodeling of a house. Picture if you will an old decaying house sitting on a luxurious piece of property. There is lush green grass as far as you can see. However, in order to bring restoration to the house it must be gutted and possibly even torn down to the very foundation. If the foundation is strong, then it can remain and be rebuilt upon. If not, even the foundation must be laid again!

So it is with lives that have been built on unstable foundations and/or false truths, (including any wounded or bruised emotions). In order to restore the house, you must get to the very root of the problem, which will require tearing down false concepts before re-structuring can occur. Then the healing process can begin.

The Holy Spirit of God is awesome at restructuring old buildings. He sees our worth, even when we can't, and rolls up His sleeves and with great joy, works us both to will and to do of His good pleasure.

There's also a time to weep and a time to laugh, a time to mourn, and a time to dance. Let me stop here and interject a truth, "tears are for cleansing." So men, if you never weep or if you think it's unmanly to cry, then you'll never be fully cleansed or healed. There is "healing" in tears. Unfortunately some men have been told that men don't cry and to suppress their emotions. The truth though is that it's not a sign of weakness, but a human emotion.

Jesus was 100% God and 100% man, and he cried. The shortest verse in the Bible says, "Jesus wept." So, there is a time for weeping and a time for laughing! They both have their place. Remember, laughter does good like a medicine, but a sad countenance dries up the bones. I know this to be true! At one point in my life I had really become secluded, isolated from others and very sad. I withdrew from those whom I loved and loved me, and found little to laugh about. Days drew on routinely and each day was lonesome and difficult. During this time my bones literally were drying up and deteriorating. Even my strength was weak. But, when laughter and joy came as a result of me opening up and interacting with others, I found my health being restored and my bones feeling stronger!

There's a time for everything under the heaven. There's a time to gather stones and a time to cast them away. In the Hebrew language stone means "to build." There's a time to embrace and a time to refrain from embracing, a time to get and a time to lose, a time to keep and a time to cast away (or give away), a time to tear and a time to sew, a time to be silent (a wise man knows when to be silent), and a time to speak, a time to love and a time to hate, a time for war and a time for peace.

Each one of these times comes in a particular season. If you live long enough, over the course of your years you will probably experience them all. So in consideration of all of this the wise preacher asks, "What then does it profit a man for all his labor or toil under the sun?" He says, I've watched it all, it's painful exerting busy-ness, and labor that man chooses to exercise day in and day out. **Man does not consider that God has already made everything beautiful in its time, and put in every man's heart and mind the knowledge of him**. He has put eternity in each man, yet no man can find out all that God has done from the beginning to the end.

Seeing all this and that God has planned everything and knows the end from the beginning and every detail of our lives, we ought to be glad, enjoy the life he has given us and do good. This includes enjoying the good of all our labor, for this too is God's gift.

We know (are assured) that whatever God does, it lasts forever and we cannot add or take away one thing from it. Why does God do this? So that men will worship him and reverently fear him. It is his desire that man knows and understands that He is God, who loves each man and desires to have an intimate loving lasting relationship with each of us. Yes, you are special to God! You are highly significant and extremely important. He took the time to specifically preorder your plan, not leaving out one detail.

Jeremiah 29:11 says, "For I know the plans I have for you, plans to prosper you and not to harm you, plans to do you good; plans to give you a hope and a future, to bring you to an expected end." God's plans include you, and every man, woman, boy and girl who has ever lived and ever will live.

There is nothing new under the sun; what has been, shall be again, and what is now has already been. In a sense, history really does repeat itself. Rulers have come and gone and some have had the same principles and concepts.

I was praying for my family, crying out to God on their behalf with strong prayers, fasting and intercession, when he directed me to Psalms 50. Moses who was interceding for the children of Israel wrote this psalm. I almost fell off my chair as I read some of the same exact petitions I had just placed before the Lord!

I said, "God, Moses' prayer is the same as mine!" I was astonished, to say the least.

However, now I realize that there really isn't anything new under the sun. Also, like Moses, I too shall die someday and move on and someone will take my place. In fact, the Master already predetermined it. This someone will take what I am doing to the next level, the next season, the next place in God. So in light of this, I have decided to trust him totally, and to live a life of joy and peace in Him without fear or worry! Will you join me in reverential worship and obey Him. Know that He has all things planned.

Our job is to just say, "Yes, Lord, I agree with you, and then do what he says, keep his commands to Love Him and to love others. Worship God in your heart, and with your mouth.

This leads to a stress free life without worry or concern. All of my life I'd been a worrier controlled by the "what ifs" – what if this happens, or that happens negatively. Once this stressful way of life almost killed me! I had lived my life under so much stress until one day I actually laid dying in my bed. At which time I heard the still small voice of God within me say, "I shall not die, but live and declare the works of the Lord." It jarred my soul and impacted my life forever! I also remember my husband and children being all around me, and my husband praying for me to live.

As he prayed I felt life and strength flow all through my body, almost like being hooked up to intravenous. The instant he let go, though, I felt my inner self drifting away. The moment he left the room, my wall became a movie screen, and I saw the many works of my life before me, most of which were being burned in a huge fire! Only a few of the good things I'd done in life remained. I knew instantly that what had burned were those things I'd done out of an insincere heart, to be seen of men. Even though they were things I'd done in church, they weren't for God's glory but mine. At that time I was the superintendent of Sunday School, a deaconess, church secretary, and much more.

I heard God's voice say, "Anita, are you ready to go? What do you want to do?" I said, "Lord I want to live and declare your works. I want to see my kids grown up and I want to do things from this day on that you direct which bring glory to you only!"

Soon the paramedics arrived! As they wheeled me out to the ambulance, a lady came running down the street to me screaming, "Anita, you shall not die but live and declare the works of the Lord!" This lady was a part of a divine appointment. Those words so jarred my soul until I hung onto the promises of them, repeating them over and over all the way to the hospital. Even though the enemy had sowed years of negative stress in my life, and I had made some unwise choices that put me in adverse situations, God still was going to fulfill his good plans for me. So, needless to say, I live today and declare the works of the Lord. God has been extremely faithful to me!

This incident in my life, (although it holds much significance and many memories for me), would be meaningless to you unless I stepped back and related to you the events that led up to this state of stress. God had been speaking to me continuously to let go of the things that caused stress. He said that it would kill me. I, however, didn't know how to let go! I would let go for a season and then take it all back again.

From a child through adulthood, I lived in fear of the "what ifs." Having gone through much turmoil, it taught me to be on the edge, worrying and expecting bad things to happen, instead of good. At the age of 15 I began to question God's purpose for my life. Was it to be constantly filled with turmoil, stress, and uncertainty? How could I make all this pain and confusion go away? Is this what you meant for my life? If so, it doesn't make any sense!

Finally, one day I felt I could take the pressure no longer, so I ran secretly into the dark bathroom and screamed out to the God I could not see! At the height of my frustrations, not knowing what to do, I heard his kind voice speak to me, saying, "Anita, put your hand in my hand. I will never leave you nor forsake you!" As I looked in the direction of that voice, I saw on the wall of my dark bathroom, a shadow of an arm and hand with a hole in it, blood streaming down from it. However, still unable to comprehend that He really could and would take care of my situations, I cried out from the depth of my soul, "Lord, please tell me the truth. If you say this, please don't let me down!" He gently repeated, "I will never leave you nor forsake you." Then he said, "I love you, Anita." Instantly I felt peace like never before. For me, that day began a walk of trust and trying to let go of stress.

For many years after, He continued to say, "Trust Me." Well, it was a struggle, since I'd only known very few men I could trust. So, as a grown woman, after years and years of this worry and fear, my body collapsed, rendering me helpless and unable to move! My body began to lose its ability to function and my brain couldn't make my arms and legs move. Neither could my mouth speak the thoughts I heard in my head. Even the simplest things like bathing, dressing, combing my hair, and brushing my teeth became impossible tasks for me.

Imagine me, a woman who always did things for herself, now being bathed and dressed by my family. Even in this time, I believe God allowed me to learn some things about the love of others and the need for others in my life. I've always been a giver, but now I was learning to receive.

I remember one day after I'd come home from the hospital looking out of my kitchen window with tears in my eyes (a time to weep) and crying unto God! I couldn't even wash something as simple as a cup that was in my sink! I cried for healing! It didn't manifest instantly, but gradually it happened.

Why am I saying all of this? It's so you can fully understand and totally comprehend that God is in charge, and that there is a time for everything. Don't get stressed out and don't live in fear or worry any longer! This is the enemy's plan to kill you before your appointed time to die. Rather, trust God and do good, keep his commands which are to love Him totally with all of your being, and love one another as Jesus has loved us. Laugh and be joyful in all things. Even the Apostle Paul from his prison cell wrote, "Rejoice in the Lord always: and again I say Rejoice."(Phil. 4:4) He goes on to say in verses 6-7 to live in the peace of God.

God sees, knows, and hears all and has already set a time to judge the righteous and the wicked. The wicked man may appear to be getting away with his wickedness without judgment, but know for certain that he is not. There will be a day of reckoning with God. What you see now is his longsuffering and his great mercy being extended. He's giving the wicked a chance to repent.

It is so important for us to live the way God has ordained because this is a proving ground. Our lives here are for the purpose of separating the wheat from the tares, or in layman's terms, separating those who will love and honor God from those who will not. He says that eye hath not seen, ear hath not heard, neither hath it entered into the heart of man, (no man that has ever lived); the things that God has prepared for them that love him. Hold onto your hats, folks; there is more to come! God has additional plans for us after this life on earth is completed and only God knows exactly what they are.

In conclusion, honor God, reverence him, love and worship him, and do things His way! For without God you are lost and will become similar to the beasts of the earth. The same things that happen to them happen to men who live apart from God; in the end they both die. All return to the dust of the earth and shall never see life on earth again. This man shall be separated from God eternally, and he shall never know good again.

Food For Thought

1. Do you understand the difference between a time and a season? There is a difference.

   - A season normally encompasses a series of times. For those of us who are visual learners, let me explain it pictorially using an open umbrella. The umbrella represents a season. Notice that when opened, you see various points on the umbrella. Let's say each of these points represent a specific time.

   - Each time has within it an event or events that have been clearly laid out by the Master (God), including divine appointments, circumstances, and situations. Just as, when the rain (in the natural) falls to the earth, it has a time of beginning, endurance, and ending, so also the seasons that God sends us.

2. What season do you believe you are in right now? How can you be assured of fulfilling all the appointed times and seasons?

3. Make a list of the things you have in your heart to do, even if they seem unattainable. Phil. 4:13 says, "I can do all things through Christ which strengthens me."

Now go before God in prayer, talk with Him, and receive His plan for each of these desires. Next, put it into action. Don't procrastinate. Procrastination is an enemy of destiny. You are going to excel in each area God has placed in your heart. Why? He is the Master with the "master plan". He designed the blueprint for your life.

Chapter Four
<u>LIFE'S BALANCE</u>

Solomon after considering all the work done here on earth began to see the inadequacies of man. He observed that those who are oppressed have no one to comfort them and ironically their oppressors had no one either, just power. However, even in their power they were empty, **for power and prestige can never fill a void**. So he concluded that it was better for the one not yet born than for those who are alive because the unborn have never seen nor known evil.

He also saw that a man's neighbor envies him when he does right work. The neighbor never considers that the man had to travail or work diligently to produce this work and the benefits thereof. It is so vain (or empty) to envy someone else, instead, work diligently with your hands and produce results that bring satisfaction from your labors.

Only a person without understanding or a foolish person will fold his hands, refusing to work, and expect to receive the same results as he who works. In doing this, he shall die without ever achieving his full potential, never knowing or entering into his divine purpose and without any fruit from his time here on earth. How tragic this would be. I can only imagine how this breaks the heart of God to see his most precious creation, the one created in his image, never producing like fruit.

Please know that even in this working with our hands, it is better to have a small portion with quietness and peace, than to have a large portion with much weariness over unnecessary bills, expenses, and worldly cares! **The most important thing is that we are diligent and do those things that God sets before us.** Then the blessings will find you! The writer says that it is so sad to see someone who is working day and night, night and day, and yet is all alone without friend or family member to share it with. This person just works, works, works, never ceases at any time and even deprives himself of precious sleep and social pleasures. He never stops to think why he is doing this, or to whom he will leave all of his gain? Solomon says that this too is vain and a horrible state to be in.

Do you know anyone like this? I do. I've watched people lose precious years by being driven by their work. They'd work hundreds of hours a week with no time for God or others. What's the use of doing this? Is it for the money? What good is it to earn all this and be too exhausted to enjoy life? One day you wake up all alone and realize how futile this had all been.

It is better if there are two people, rather than one person because there is someone to share this with. Consequently, if one of you were to fall the other would help him up. But who is there to help the one that is alone? And if there are two, (a husband and wife for example, or two friends), one can help the other up.

Think about even the provision of body heat for the other in the cold winter season. If alone, it is truly impossible to provide that extra body heat when it's cold. I remember the cold winter nights when my husband and I would snuggle up together to stay warm and toasty! I always had cold feet and eventually they would find their way to his side of the bed. Sometimes he would allow me the privilege of warming them on his warm, toasty body, and "hooray" "instant heat!" Since his death or as I choose to say, transition to heaven, my feet are oh so cold in the winter – so I have found a replacement, a heating pad. What a horrible way to keep your feet warm!!! So, I too conclude that two are better than one in many ways.

Now, this is especially true in the midst of a disagreement. If someone comes against you in great opposition and you have someone standing with you on your side, the odds are changed (there is now two against one). If there are three people (for instance family members) than that chord cannot easily be broken. As a child getting into a fight, if the person came at me with a family member or friend, I'd say it was unfair. Why? Because it was two against one, double the strength and double the power. So it is with you when you have someone to share with you in your everyday experience, whether working, socializing, sleeping, eating, or whatever. God made us to be with others. No man has ever or will ever fulfill his purpose on earth without others to help and share in it. In fact, purpose is all about helping others. So be kind and friendly, and see all men after Christ. **Treat ever person as if he were Christ, and watch how your life changes**.

Solomon also instructs us to walk in wisdom every day. Be wise. The Bible says that if you lack wisdom, ask God and he will give it to you in abundance. For a poor, yet wise child is better than an old or elderly king who is foolish. This king will not be admonished or praised anymore because he foolishly spends the people's money through unwise decisions, so that even he that is born in his kingdom becomes poor. But watch how that poor, yet wise child comes out of financial prison to reign. Why? Wisdom will teach you how to increase and how to maintain what you receive. If you are foolish, however, even what you receive you will utterly spend unwisely and become poor.

The finality of chapter four says that after considering all of this and observing all the people who lived in Solomon's days, and knowing that there is no end to the increase of people who will be born on the earth, how futile is all of this vanity. For one shall come after you are dead and assume ownership of all your labors, and in most cases, shall not rejoice in you or do it the same way you do. Why? He shall have his own way of doing things. So in light of all of this know that this is also vain or empty and vexing or disturbing of spirit.

I interpret what is being said to mean, "Enjoy the life God has given you; do all things unto him, and be not overzealous in any area. Know your purpose and why you are doing what you are doing. Never do things for recognition of man, for who is man; it is God whom you must please. Forget about laboring in vain (without purpose) and chasing after this world's gain; instead seek God's purpose and go after Him. Don't be a fool and refuse to work or labor, but don't work so much that you don't take time to be happy, enjoying life and fellowshipping with family and friends."

I believe God is telling us to live a balanced life! **After all, when you're finished here on earth, someone else will take over where you left off and he will have his own agenda, not yours!** So, take time to enjoy the people and things God has surrounded you with. Admire the beauty of your surroundings no matter where you are, and most of all spend quality time talking and fellowshipping with God, getting his viewpoint on things, and his wisdom, pray daily for his perfect will to be done in earth just like it is in heaven. Go about doing good, just like God. Enjoy your life here and make it more enjoyable for others whenever possible, for in comparison to eternity, it is but a **moment** in time! (What will you do with your "Moment?")

Food For Thought

1. **Take a moment to fill out the Life's Balance Chart. Which areas are out of order?**

2. **What will you do to remedy this?**

3. **Taking time to share and enjoy the seasons of this life with others is a necessity. Use a blank calendar and schedule in that time. Did you remember to schedule in your time to be alone with God? Is He 1st in your life?**

Chapter Five

REVERENTIAL FEAR OF GOD

As a child growing up I was taught to reverence, or hold a special regard for the house of God. The old folks used to say, "This is God's house; God lives here!" When we'd enter the door of the sanctuary, we had to respect God's house and only talk about things that would please Him. Now we know that God is too large to live in a house; he is everywhere at all times present! God says that heaven is his throne and the earth his footstool. Yet, he allowed King Solomon (David's son) to build him a house.

I believe that what Solomon is saying in Chapter 5 is that when your feet enter the house of God, be reverent. Be more ready to hear than to constantly talk. He says that just like when you are so busy during the day until at night you can't enter into a comfortable sleep because of much dreaming, so also is the person who is always talking. You talk so much until you say foolish things, even uttering a vow before God that you can't fulfill. But, it's better not to vow a vow than to make a vow and break it.

So, no matter how much you are pressured to make that vow, if you are not going to keep it, don't make it. It's better to make a vow with a pure, sincere heart, knowing that you are going to keep it, than to make one and break it.

Better yet, just reverence God in all things. If you vow a vow, then keep it. But I believe it is better to just let your "yes" be yes and your "no" be no. With this God is pleased! The Word of God says that the promises of God are "yes" and "amen" to the glory of God. So, be like God; if it's yes, then so be it (amen).

God knows everything and we should honor Him as King. **He gives us wisdom to know what is right and what is wrong and the power to obey Him**. When it comes to making decisions in life, He has put wisdom in our hearts and the ability to know the right time to make each decision. For me this is very significant. This is an area of my life that I've struggled with, not necessarily should I or shouldn't I, but mostly the timing of a thing. Making a decision and having it to be my final one was always hard. I'd always think, "What if this isn't the right one or the right time to do it. Seeing the picture for others seemed obvious, but seeing it for myself, it has always been filled with questions. Somehow the "What if's" entered my mind. I had a lack of confidence and also multiple insecurities. Looking from the outside you'd never have guessed it, but in my mind they existed.

I was liberated by time in God's presence just talking with Him and meditating upon His Word. It's actually one of my favorite things to do. Hearing from Him and getting His direction truly fascinates me! Then I'm confronted with my next step, when to act?

I spent so much time thinking about the "when" aspect, that confusion would set in and then delay. Normally, I'd have to be almost forced out of the current situation into God's next step for me. I've since learned to put my faith and confidence in God and rely on His ability in me to accomplish what He has designed.

When going through one of these times, God used my spiritual daughter Robyn Arheghan to give me a scripture that opened my eyes and brought clarity to this entire thing. She told me to read Ecclesiastes 8:5, which says, "Whosoever observes the (King's) command will experience no harm, and a wise man's <u>mind</u> will know both <u>when</u> and <u>what</u> <u>to</u> <u>do</u>." Then verse 6 says, "For every purpose and matter has its (right) time and <u>judgment,</u> although the misery and wickedness of man lies heavily upon him (who rebels against the King!)"

This taught me that I can make decisions and follow them through. My heart (inner self) will direct my way. All I have to do is do what I know (understand) to do. Listen and obey God. Do what's right without delay. **This scripture brought me out of a hole I'd been in all my life.**

Also, in this chapter we are instructed not to be astonished or surprised by the oppression of the poor and the judgment and justice being perverted in the land, but rather know that **God sees all**. You know for me this really struck home. I have always had a heart for the poor and for those who I feel are many times forgotten or looked over and insignificant or unimportant. But in reading this, I understood that God sees everything and he is in charge and he will enable us to provide for the poor and also bring judgment and justice where necessary. He watches everything and will repay and bless those who remember the poor and deliver them from their oppressors. He blesses the work of our hands so we in turn can reach out to the poor and bring the gospel and the physical things they need.

We know that God has given the earth to us for everyone to profit from. He has not given some the ability to profit and others not. No, for that would be unjust and he is righteous. So, as the old folks would say, if we put our hands to the plow we can produce. God says that he has given us the power to get wealth. This doesn't say that he has given us wealth, but rather the power (ability/wisdom) to get wealth. There's something we must do. Faith without works is dead. So we must use our faith together with our works and get wealth. The scripture says that this is true for everyone. Even the king is served by the same fields as we are.

Remember though in your profiting, if you love money you are not going to be satisfied with it. Neither will he that loves abundance be satisfied, for the more he increases the more he desires! Why? Because the more you acquire the more responsibility it brings with it. Don't you know that even the number of people increase who are under your care? (Somehow, wealth attracts people.)

God loves us to have things and to enjoy the things he gives us, as long as the things don't have us. In other words, keep it all in proper perspective. Remember that things are temporal and fade away, but God is eternal and everlasting. Always keep him first!

It is better to labor with your hands and enjoy what you have, than to get gain dishonestly and become rich apart from God. At least the honest laborer can sleep peacefully whether he has little or much. But the man that does not know or honor God can't sleep for fear that someone will try to get his wealth! Night and day he is preoccupied with his fear of losing his wealth and/or how to get more!

This is a sad picture; he can't sleep for worrying over his increase. He never considers that after his death someone else will enjoy the fruit of his increase. It's not unusual for that person to be so concerned with his riches until he hordes it. He never uses it for its intended purposes, but rather for evil gain. Because his motives are evil, God will not bless it, so that even the son born to him shall not enjoy the fruit. Man is born into this world naked (without any material things), and shall go out the same way. Since all of this is true, how shall we live and conduct our lives before God Almighty, our Creator!

Integrity

Years ago contracts were sealed with a handshake and a promise. Your word was your bond. You could trust their word. God is the same yesterday, today, and forever. When He gives us a promise, He keeps it.

Another area of integrity is with money. God gave you the power to get wealth. A better word for power is "ability"

Food For Thought

1. Take a moment to evaluate your life. Can people bank on your word?
2. Can they trust you to follow through?
3. Are you utilizing the gifts within you and being diligent and consistent?
4. Have you created a business plan to achieve the goals God has placed in you?
5. Is there a desire in your heart to start a business, ministry, etc… but you need more clarity? Spend time with God and develop a plan.
6. Who can you seek out to mentor/coach you in this area?
   - If you could not answer yes to questions 1-5 then, take some time alone with God and ask for His help.

- If you did answer yes to these questions, are you consistent? Your "yes" should mean yes and your "no" should mean no.

- Experts say that change normally takes 21 days of consistent, positive behavior in order to take effect. So remember, it's a process, and God has given you time.

Chapter 6

HANDLING NOTARITY

"What to Do With the Fame and Favor"

Fame is conditional and temporal. Fame, unlike favor, is dependent upon how well known you are not how well liked you are. There are multitudes of people who have experienced fame or notoriety, but have not been liked by a major part of society. So fame is not dependent upon how well liked you are, but the fact that you are noticed. Your peers celebrate you, for a designated period of time, or a season.

I've seen a sad thing happen to many passing through fame's portals. During their time of fame they have become so overwhelmed with the notoriety until they have forgotten to live life itself and have begun to live for the notoriety or fame. In an effort to maintain this exuberant feeling of acceptance and honor, they have sold their souls!

You say, how? Since fame is conditional, and temporal, it is fleeting. Anything fleeting is slipping out of your hands or getting away from you. I liken the pursuit of fame to chasing after the wind. Wind, unlike other substances, cannot be caught, neither put in a bottle to be kept for a later period of time. So if fame comes to you or notoriety increases, put no faith in it, for it, unlike Christ, is fleeting.

Jesus, Himself, experienced fame; the Bible says that his fame went out all over! People began to notice him for various reasons, some because of the miracles he did, others for the words he spoke, and the religious community for the upset he caused in their political arena!

In some regions he was celebrated and in others hated for the very things others celebrated him. However, he left on record the key to mastering fame. It's found in John 2:23-25, which says "Now when he was in Jerusalem at the Passover in the feast day, many believed in his name, when they saw the miracles which he did. **But Jesus did not commit himself unto them** because he knew all men and needed not that any should testify of him: **for he knew what was in man**." The word "knew" in the Hebrew is yada which means to perceive, be acquainted with.

There was nothing in man; he knew man's weakness and failure. Jesus understood that man would praise him today and curses him tomorrow, depending upon the situation. Man's praise would be based upon his like or dislike of what Jesus said and did, on how it affected him personally. Therefore Jesus did not commit himself to any. He did not allow himself to be absorbed in or swayed at any time by their praise or criticism.

This is a very important key to fame. **Do Not Allow Yourself To Be Entangled With The Popularity Of The People – Don't Become Wrapped Up In Their Praise Or Condemnation.** Otherwise you'll never accomplish anything.

I find that at the heart of the desire to be well known or praised by man is actually a root of pride. Isn't it ironic how "pride puffs up, and love humbles." Ask yourself, "Why do I want to be noticed? Why must I be celebrated? Why do I desire the attention and/or applause of men? Why do I desire to hear men speak well of me?" God's word on the other hand says for us to be leery when all men speak well of us.

You know, I had to ask myself these self same questions many times and then answer them. I loved it when people thought I was wonderful – superwoman! All my life I wanted the applause and attention of others, whether trying to outshine everyone at cheerleading, leading the band as the drum majorette, being a super wife and flawless mother, and yes even aspiring to be a dynamic teacher/preacher of the gospel! However, **Jesus said, "And I, if I be lifted up will draw all men unto me."** So, why did I desire to hear my name? It was that ugly pride that needed to be removed. I had to realize that it's not about me. It's about the one who deserves all the praise, honor, and glory – Jesus Christ! He gave his life for us on Calvary's cross. He is the only sacrifice for man's sins and through His blood alone we have forgiveness of sins. Through acceptance of him as our Lord and Savior we experience God's grace as sons and daughters. **So if we are going to applaud someone, let us applaud Him.**

If we need to be celebrated by others, we're in bad shape. The beauty is we can go boldly before God, get in his presence and talk with him. Ask him to allow you to see and know His great love for you. Then meditate on His love in sending His Son, and all the scriptures revealing Jesus Christ. God will walk with you daily and continue to feed you on His Word. The Word is like a mirror, reflecting the image of God in you. The more you look into it, the more you become like it.

For years I repeatedly prayed, "God help me not to be prideful and guess what, I found myself continue to go through situations of prideful actions, then sorrow for being that way, trying to make amends to those I verbally hurt, and the cycle continued. Now in my heart, I really wanted to change but could not as long as I was looking at **my** imperfections. But, the moment I began looking into the perfect law of liberty (grace) and the beauty of Christ Jesus, His reflection shown in me. Before I knew it, I saw the manifestations of His work. (Ephesians 2:10) "for we are His workmanship, created in Christ Jesus unto good works which He has before ordained that we should walk in them."

The former way was painful to my flesh, and unpleasant to my mind, will, and emotions, but God's Word, cleansed me and purified my mind, giving me a new way of thinking and acting. It's like being constipated in the natural and filled with all kinds of gook that needs to come out. What do you do? If you are really clogged you take a laxative?

Isaiah 53:10-11 says, "Yet it pleased the Lord to bruise him; he hath put him to grief: when thou shalt make his soul an offering for sin, he shall see his seed, he shall prolong his days, and the pleasure of the Lord shall prosper in his hand. He shall see of the travail of his soul, and shall be satisfied: by his knowledge shall my righteous servant justify many: for he shall bear their iniquities." Only Jesus did this for us, so only he gets all the glory! Humble yourself before God and allow him to purify your heart and motives and remove all areas of pride from your life.

Pride cannot stand in God's presence of love and grace, so allow His word to liberate you. I guarantee you that your life will be more wonderful and free. The chains of pride will drop powerless to the floor and you will experience a freedom such as you have never known before.

Food For Thought

1. **What is the difference between fame and favor?**

2. **God's word says that God has given you favor with Him and all men.**

    *   **List 5 ways you can show God's favor towards someone this week. Whatever you want others to do for you, do for someone else.**

    *   **Many of us at some point in our lives have operated in pride. Sometimes we don't even know we're being prideful until later on.**

    *   **To avoid the pride trap, shine the search light on Jesus, and know that He lives within each of the Believers. "As He is, so are you in this world!"**

    *   **Take some time to read Appendix A on pride. It's interesting how different it is from humility. God will give you many opportunities to walk in love and humility. Try journaling some of them; you'll be amazed at the love of God in operation in your life, and how many lives are affected by it.**

    *

- When you become confident in God's love for you, who you are in Christ and what He's done for you, you won't need the validation of men. You won't need the applause of men. You'll walk like Christ did. Neither their applause, nor their condemnation will affect you.

Chapter 7

A GOOD NAME

Why is a good name better than precious ointment or perfume? Have you ever went into a store and sampled various brands of perfume or cologne? Years ago, the salesperson would spray a little on your wrist for you to smell. After about three or four different samples (even if it was just the oil touching your skin), you'd get confused as to which scent went with which perfume. They'd seem to blend together and produce a strong smell.

In contrast, today they spray swatches for you to smell. The more pure the perfume, the more costly it is, especially the oils. Scripture tells us of a lady who had an alabaster box of precious ointment/perfume worth about one year's wages, which she poured on Jesus. Did she know that she was anointing his body for the burial? Some of the disciples became angry at her for frivolously wasting **her** oil. Judas declared that it could have been sold and the money used to feed the poor. Jesus himself vindicated and exalted her for this kind-hearted gesture, declaring that the poor you always have with you, but he they would not. He knew that he would soon face death on the cross, the true culmination of what He was sent here for.

Other places in scripture people have been anointed for prestigious and/or high offices by the use of anointing oil. For example, Samuel anointed Saul as king and later he anointed David as king. However, the Bible clearly states that even more precious than this perfumed oil is a good name. Why? **A good name (honorable and full of integrity)**

will get you into places that the expensive perfume cannot. A good name is well known and respected by all. It can be trusted.

In Bible history, it was the customary to seal a contract with their word and the exchange of their shoe. If the person had a reputation of a being a foolish man, no one trusted his word and therefore even his shoe was valueless!

As a little girl I remember people just gave their word to each other and sealed an agreement with a handshake. If a grocer brought food to a regular customer who didn't have the means to pay him that day, he could trust him until a later date. Sure enough, on that date the customer stood on the steps of the grocer's establishment waiting for him with all the promised money in hand. He kept his word.

Today, however, this is not necessarily the case. The value of a good name in many instances has been lost and a promise to pay only means, "If I can." Many times we say, "I'll try my best" and have well-meaning intentions, but don't follow through. Soon our name can no longer be trusted. Therefore sometimes lending institutions now require a co-signer or someone whose name they can trust.

I know for myself that time past I made purchases on credit that I really hadn't sat down and counted the cost. Therefore, I found myself in the midst of debt beyond my ability to pay in the time frame agreed. In other words, I dug myself into a whole deeper than my ability to climb out, and through this ruined "a good name." So then began the tedious, time consuming repairing process. **Know this, wisdom stands at the gate of every decision and speaks to each of us.** We will either listen and do as instructed, or bypass wisdom, as we whisk past the gate and into the adventure!

Wisdom says, "It's better to have a good name than the precious perfume." It's better to maintain your good name than to acquire things or positions until you're ready for them.

It seems as though in the midst of talking about a good name, King Solomon changes thoughts and begins to talk about the day of one's death being better than one's birth; but in reality he is actually continuing the previous thought. He says that when you first enter this world through birth you have no idea of what lies ahead. You have neither accumulated wisdom nor gained understanding in the affairs of this life. You are just embarking upon your journey and adventures still await you in the valley of the unknown.

In contrast, at the end of your life, you should leave with much wisdom and understanding carrying forth a good name and reputation to be honored by all. That's why he says; it's better to go to a house of mourning than a house of feasting. At the house of mourning the eulogy will honor your good name. Hopefully the things the preacher will say about you will be true! Have you ever attended a funeral of someone you knew and when the time came for the eulogy (words said about the person's life) you wondered who the preacher was speaking about? Had they exchanged this person's body for another's?

Seriously though, sometimes we exaggerate about a person in order to give him a good name at his departure. Don't let this be the case with you. Live your life honestly and respectfully so that men will honor your good name and not feel compelled to make up something good about you.

What's in the house of feasting – laughter! Everyone loves to laugh, and laughter does good like a medicine, but he says that at times sorrow is better. Why? Laughing about a good joke brings joy, but as soon as the laugh is over, sometimes the joy fades away. It's possible to be upset or depressed and laugh at a joke, and then return to your state of sadness or heaviness of heart. However, when a person experiences sorrow for sin, after hearing the word of God at a funeral, he repents and his heart is made free. This man then gains a great understanding and true gladness. So embrace the rebuke of the wise (he who possess wisdom) rather than the song of fools.

God equates the laughter of fools to the irritations of hearing thorns crackling under a pot. It's annoying and gets on your nerves! You wish that it would just stop, or they'd just be quiet! It is so empty.

What are some of the things that bring down a wise man and make him foolish? They are oppression, extortion, and a bribe. These all destroy and altar a wise man's judgment and his understanding. If he can be bought, he can fall! That's why it's so important to be free from all idols, and free from covetousness. An idol is anything that turns your heart away from God (partially or fully). Strong's Concordance says it's an earthen vessel; painful toil; an image (i.e., for worship); a heathen god (or the worship of such).

The Hebrew word for worship is "shachah" which means, "to depress, i.e., prostrate in homage to royalty or God; to bow (self) down; crouch; fall down (flat); humbly beseech, do (make) obeisance; to reverence; make to stoop, worship. Therefore, an idol is anything or anyone that occupies the place in your heart that is reserved for God, such as your job, family member or friend, material possessions, positions of authority or prominence (whether in church or in the world), and the like.

Let's talk about covetousness. Paraphrase Webster's dictionary, covetousness is enviously longing for something another person has. It is to burn passionately with greed for something or someone. It's what you think of when you go to bed at night and the first thing on your mind when you wake up in the morning! If it is really ingrained in you, you will even find yourself constantly dreaming about it or them. No, these dreams are not from God, but rather from the burning lust that dwells within you. – Get free from them! Denounce those gods/idols in the Name of Jesus; be free to love and worship God Almighty and Him alone. He said in His Word, "Thou shalt have no (No) other gods before me. I am a jealous God."

I caution you to recognize that these things present themselves in your life as snares to bring you down. Satan will use them against you. The Bible says to lie not against the truth. Rather, confess it to God and allow His precious Holy Spirit to set you free.

All it takes is repentance and a turning away from them and going in the opposite direction. God promises in II Chronicles 7:14, that if we, his people, who are called by His name, will humble ourselves and pray, seek his face, and turn from our wicked ways, then he will hear from heaven, forgive our sins and heal our land. What an awesome promise and invitation to come to him; he's waiting to liberate and give freedom. He alone knows your end from your beginning.

Better is the end of a thing than the beginning. It's easier to look back and recognize how all the puzzle pieces of your life have fit together, than to start out not knowing what lies ahead. Seeing we don't know where everything goes and can't even tell what tomorrow holds, then just be patient, relax. Trust that God (who knows all things) is in control. What would it profit you to be proud and haughty seeing you also must wait until tomorrow to experience tomorrow? **Therefore, it's better to be patient and relaxed than to be proud and high minded!**

This reminds me of an earlier part of my life. I was born the second child of five and sandwiched between two brothers whom I dearly love and admire. When growing up, they used to tell me that I was "high minded" and thought I was above everybody else.

I'd argue them down that I was not (as I continued to hold my nose high in the air)! I'd say that I was just like everybody else! In our state there lived a very wealthy and influential family named the Duponts who owned much in the state, and there was also a part of the city that was not as ritzy, or prestigious. In this area was a street called "Front Street". So they'd tell me that I had a "Dupont mind and a Front Street pocketbook." I'd get so mad at them every time they'd say this and insist that I was not this way at all!

Years later, after I'd married and birthed my children, one day someone very close to me said something very profound. It was, "You think you are better than they are!" (It was the fact that I acted as if I was so much better.) I was immediately reminded of my childhood days and knew that I was displaying an air of pride and superiority, which had subtly taken root over the years. This was many years before I began to understand God's grace and mercy for us all. I went to God and asked for his help. I no longer wanted to live with a haughty attitude. The funny thing is, the basis for pride and haughtiness, only exist in the person's mind. God has made a way for us to take every thought captive. How? Casting down imaginations and every high thing that exalts itself against the knowledge of God, and bringing into captivity every thought to the obedience of Christ. (II Corinthians 10:5)

Now, I'd like to say that in one moment, like a flash of lightening it was gone, but that's not so. It had become a battle, a stronghold that took root as a child, which had to be brought down over the years through meditating on the Word. Remember we cast down every imagination that places itself against the knowledge of God (every vain imagination of my mind) and bring captive (like a prisoner in chains) my every thought

to the obedience of God, by speaking His Word on this area and eventually allowing it to

change my thoughts.

If you can relate or identify with any of this and can find an area of pride or arrogance in

your life, please deal with it quickly. Go before God immediately and allow him to free

you. I have found that pride is only a false god or idol. I once had a pastor, Dr. Gary

Whetstone, who taught me to locate the area of challenge, identify the enemy spirit

operating, and eradicate it. My mother discovered the acronym for locate, identify, and

eradicate is "lie" and this is what these demonical spirits do.

      L - Locate

      I - Identify

      E - Eradicate

Please spend a few minutes reviewing the attached appendix on pride. I guarantee that it

will be a blessing to you and a great eye opener.

Many times prideful people are hasty and full of anger, and we know that anger rests in

the heart of fools. Once God instructed me to write James 1:19-20 one hundred times.

Ironically, I began writing but then resisted doing it, citing the fact that it was too long

and too much to write at one time. One day, however, I decided to be obedient and just

do it! God's word lets us know that obedience is better than sacrifice. I must say that

these two verses have become etched in me forever, and I now find myself operating by the principles found in them. I quote, "Wherefore, my beloved brethren, let every man be swift to hear, slow to speak, and slow to wrath. For the wrath of man worketh not the righteousness of God."

Isn't it funny how pride and anger go hand in hand? If you're prideful, you feel as though you must defend yourself. It seems that this wall of pride has many building blocks including, rejection, fear, pain, abandonment, failure, to name a few. Out of this anger flows hurt filled words that cut and shred anyone who comes close enough to "upset the apple cart" so to speak. This is why God says to get rid of the anger or wrath for it doesn't work God's righteousness or right way of doing things. Rather, practice being a person who listens, hears instruction, and is slow to speak or answer. Think about what you are going to say before you say it, and if it's not necessary, don't say it.

There have been times when I have been so angry, yet want so much to be rid of it, and had no idea how to get free! It seemed that the more I wanted to be free, the harder it was. I didn't want to be angry, but in my mind I couldn't stop rehearsing or thinking about the wrong or injustice done to me. Have you ever been this way? Sometimes I think the enemy works overtime in this area! I suppose that's why God's word says, "be angry and sin not, don't let the sun go down on your anger." In other words, deal with it quickly. The longer you stay in it, the more difficult it seems to just "let go of it." Don't try to figure it out, or answer the situation right now. Just leave it, walk away and ask God for help. Funny, we try everything else first, rather than just running to God for help.

It's almost like when a child is having trouble on the playground with a bunch of bullies. He hides it from his Dad and tries to handle it himself. After he's beat up and bruised, he runs to his Dad for help. What am I saying? Dad was there all the time. He's got the wisdom for the situation, but you've just got to ask.

When you feel yourself getting angry, think, "how important is this?" "I'm not going through even a small portion of what Jesus went through for me." So, in light of this determine to forgive, pray, read the Bible, or get into an attitude of worship and praise. Begin to think on something else (rather than yourself) and you'll find that the anger leaves. In fact, many times, laugh at yourself! Just think, "you were upset over that!

This is not worth the stress on the body or the missed fellowship with God and man. God did not intend for man to carry this unnecessary stress on his body and die prematurely! Rather, determine to walk in love daily. This is a forward motion journey!

Don't look back over your life and wish for the former days, instead look ahead with great expectation, love and joy, knowing that God, who made everything seen and unseen, created you with a bright prosperous future and he knows how to bring you into the fulfillment of it.

Have you ever talked with someone that lives in their past? Their entire conversation is about what they used to do, what they used to have, or who used to be in their life.

Sometimes you even avoid them because you can almost quote "word for word" what they are going to say. They talk about old marriages, old relationships, jobs, church experiences, and all types of past events in their life. Yes, they even talk about people who are dead (perhaps died many years ago) as if they are still here. They have not yet buried them. You want to say to them, "Hey that's over," or "they left a long time ago," "they are dead," or "it's ended!"

Once when I went to see my doctor about some minor symptoms I was experiencing, after examining me and chatting for a few minutes, he asked the nurse to administer a series of tests. While she was doing this, he went next door to treat another patient who had come in with an emergency.

Since the walls were paper- thin, I heard him ask an elderly lady how long she had been experiencing these symptoms. She stated that she couldn't remember when they started. Then he asked the same question in another manner. She said that she'd been recently troubled by this and then gave him a date when it began. Well, the doctor was alarmed by the fact that it had been so long ago, and very perplexed as to why she had waited until just now to come in! He came back into the room where I was to get a calendar and took it back to have the lady show him the exact day these symptoms first began. He asked again, "you mean such and such a date?" The elderly lady then told him that it was that day, but many years ago. In her mind it was just yesterday!

Let's determine today to not spend any more time (not one more second) in your past. It's over, it's done, it's finished, and it's buried! It has absolutely No Life, and you on the other hand, have a Great Big Bright, Brilliant Future ahead of you. In fact, right now as you are reading this book, you are standing in the first day of a new life! God has afforded you an opportunity to begin a brand new adventure in him! Wisdom is standing at the gate and beckoning you to come! So, while you have life, step out, and enjoy it!

Now, come closer so I can whisper something in your ear. **"DON'T LET YOUR DEAD PAST INTERRUPT OR ABORT YOUR LIVING FUTURE."** Why? Death has no place with life! Seize this opportunity to set sail on a new adventure. It only takes the decision of your mind! So, dream big and set sail. Remember to take along wisdom to guide you in every decision.

Be wise and you'll profit knowing that wisdom is a defense just as money is a defense. Wisdom is a good source of defense, as an inheritance of money is a defense. A wise man will know what actions to take, including when, and what words to speak to whom. Wisdom, however, far exceeds money in that it gives life to those who have it.

A man with money can lose it all from one unwise decision, but a wise man will know how to increase through wise decisions, because he listens to God. Therefore, consider the word of God, who is in control of everything. He sends prosperity and adversity. So take joy when you prosper and when adversity comes, knowing he has sent both. Who can make straight what he makes crooked? "We are in His hands."

The preacher of this book further proclaims that he has seen much he does not understand. He has seen a righteous man perish in his righteousness and a wicked man that prolongs his life in wickedness. To us this seems unfair and we would want the wicked to perish quickly and the righteous to live in his righteousness. But God is over all. He doesn't want any to perish but all to come to the knowledge of the Lord Jesus Christ. God is longsuffering; however, rest assure, there is a day for the judgment of the un-repented wicked. The Word says that quickly he is ensnared or trapped, and that the Lord knows the way of the righteous, but the way of the wicked shall perish.

Remember Pharaoh, the king of Egypt, who enslaved God's people (the Israelites). He mistreated them and they (the righteous) cried out to God. God heard and sent Moses to tell Pharaoh to let his people go. Exodus 9:16 says, "and in very deed have I raised thee up, (talking to Pharaoh), for to show in thee my power: and that my name may be declared throughout all the earth." Pharaoh thought he had raised himself up, but rather it was God who did this. This wicked man didn't know that God was in charge of everything, nor that God had appointed a specific time of his demise (death), and Israel's deliverance. Exodus 14 shows where Pharaoh met his end in the Red Sea. It says that the Lord looked upon Pharaoh and his entire army in the Red Sea through a pillar of fire and a cloud, and caused the wheels of the Egyptians chariots to come off. They realized too late that God was fighting for the Israelites. Even their attempt to flee was fruitless. The Lord God caused the waters to come over them, drowning them and their horses. Let me add this footnote – rest assured – the Lord knows how to save the righteous out of the hand of the wicked!

Also cease being in a hurry to be promoted and be the head over a lot of things and people! Stop striving or you can die an early death. Let God raise you up and promote you in his appointed time. I am also speaking here of being exalted over a lot of well meaning functions, including church functions. Ask yourself why you desire to be on every committee, every board, and in every boat that sails! Are you lacking attention or praise? Life becomes so much simpler when we give God the opportunity to tell us what he wants us involved in and place us in the positions he has chosen for us.

In my years of living and interacting with people in various capacities, I've learned a few things about people. They will praise you today and curse (dislike or be disappointed with) you tomorrow, so don't look for the applause of men. Look for the "well done" from God. And remember not to take it to heart when you hear someone say something negative about you, ignore it and forgive him. I'm sure that you and I alike have at one time or another said something negative about someone else. "For all have sinned and come short of the glory of God." Let's make a commitment to enjoy our lives, families, friends, and all who God brings us in contact with as we partner together in God's Kingdom and pursue peace. Leave off endeavors to be wise in your own eyes. Only God knows the future and daily gives us enough wisdom for that day!

King Solomon (the Preacher) in his attempt to understand everything applied himself to know the ins and outs of wisdom. He searched out and sought the reason for things, including the wickedness of foolishness. As a result of his findings, his understanding caused him to believe that more bitter than death is the woman whose heart is snares or traps, and if you please God you will escape her (since she only traps those void of understanding). King Solomon had 300 wives and 700 concubines which totals 1,000 women in his harem.

I suppose after looking back over his life and all the 1,000+ women, his word of warning is to stay away from her! He says that her mouth speaks smoothly and of great satisfying love, but her heart is filled with deceit, jealousy, anger, and the grave! Wow, what a strong statement. You will have given your "substance" or "strength" to a harlot who cares nothing about you, but rather about herself.

Proverbs says not to go her way! Run and run fast! Have you ever seen a rabbit run into a trap intentionally? No! Learn a lesson from the rabbit. You may say, "I'm not a rabbit, I'm more like a strong bear or roaring lion." However, even these animals are not stupid! RUN!!! Men her heart is a snare and her hands are bands or chains. She wants everything you have, including your worship, your strength, and your entire life!

Earlier in the book we stated, "The end of a thing is better than the beginning." Well, here the writer, after ending of his search for madness says that "nothing" in all the world so seduces a man and turns him away from God as an idolatrous woman. It's worse than death. She catches the man and holds him in chains (or bondage) for a lifetime. Death is an end to this present life, but this woman's snare has no end; it holds its victim captive for his entire life. One upright man, says King Solomon, has he found among a thousand, but he has not been able to find one upright woman in all the 1,000 in his harem. (His search encompassed idolatrous women, not righteous women.)

Somehow, I can't resist the urge to take a pause break here. King Solomon, permit me to say some words of wisdom concerning righteous women. There are some upright women in God's Kingdom. There are women who love the Lord and are sold out and committed to his godly rule and righteous living.

Now women, the only way the men will know that you are godly is by the reflection of Christ in you. It does matter how we carry ourselves. Our conversation should be chaste, moderate, kind, and seasoned with love. We must operate in God's right way of doing things and not the world's ways, dressing and carrying ourselves appropriately, not according to this world's trends, but according to God's principles and the leading of the Holy Spirit.

When you look in a mirror does your outfit look "hot?" Can you imagine men's heads turning and them drooling as you walk by? Are you intentionally seducing men and even finding pleasure in it? Then, this is not godly and is rather the behavior King Solomon was referring to with the harlots.

Remember ladies, he who finds a wife finds a good thing and obtains favor of the Lord. God will cause him to find you. Just do your part and be a godly woman. Look good, feel good and walk holy and uprightly before God and he'll cause you to be found. "No good thing will He withhold from he who walks uprightly before him." God will put you in the right place at the right time, just like Ruth with Boaz. He said to her, "All the city of my people know that you are a virtuous woman." (Ruth 3:11)

Men, God has a beautiful, godly wife for you. If you are not married and want to be married, ask God. He created marriage, so why not go to the one who created and instituted it. He puts a man and woman together and blesses their union. Amos 3:3 says, "Can two walk together except they agree?" God knows whom you can walk in agreement with and who can walk in agreement with you. Align yourself with God; come into agreement with Him and His Word, then He'll put you together with someone he has created to compliment you.

Now, if you are already married, I suggest you go to God for answers daily. Men love your wives as Christ loves the church. Women, love, honor and obey your husbands as Sarah did Abraham, who even called him Lord. God can knit your hearts together as you seek him, turn from your wicked (or unjust) ways, and humble yourself and pray. God promises to hear from heaven, forgive your sins, and heal your land (in this case, your marriage if it's in trouble). I encourage you to talk with God and commit your marriage into His hands. He must be that third person in it in order for it to succeed and be all he has purposed it to be. Over the years of biblical counsel to couples, I've noticed that in the church body the divorce rate among Christians has risen even higher! Some feel they are no longer compatible or no longer going in the same direction. Doctrines of devils have been released in these end times to deceive. We must pray for one another and all those going through this extremely painful situation, those who are living in unrest and hurt.

It divides what he has put together and causes great pain, hurt, rejection and totally disrupts and sometimes destroys the lives of those involved. I pray you will seek God's wisdom, fast and pray! God has a very specific wonderful plan -- seek him for answers. He has given us an open invitation to come to Him if we lack wisdom and he will give it to us liberally (a lot), and not ask for it back.

King Solomon concludes that God made man (men and women) upright, but man (through evil intentions, pride, hardness of his heart) has sought out many evils.

Food For Thought

1. What do you think of your name (reputation)?

2. What do you believe others think? (As a man thinks so shall it be. It's important what "you" think about you.

3. Now look at your life. Have you grown in areas? List these areas of growth. (Sometimes we can't see growth in our own lives and therefore don't celebrate the new person we've become. It's easier to see growth in others rather than ourselves.

4. Can you identify "strongholds" in your life that still need to be brought down? Remember these are mindsets that hinder our progress or growth.

- Isn't it funny that all these take place in our minds. They are only thoughts (seeds) but if allowed to stay there, they germinate, grow roots, and produce fruit. Then we act out what we think.

- Remember the solution: L – Locate

  I – Identify

  E - Eradicate

- Ask God, The Holy Spirit, to help you identify these strongholds and to be free of them. Also, it's good to have another person agree with you in prayer. Then take actions. Read all the scriptures associated with this and begin to meditate on them daily. Cast down imaginations (in your mind) that exalt themselves against the knowledge of God, and bring into captivity <u>every</u> <u>thought</u> to obey God. (In other words, if the thought or image is different from God's Word, then reject it!) And remember, "you are the righteousness of God in Christ Jesus.

Chapter Eight

The Key is Wisdom

Wisdom is the key to everything. It's the key to life. Therefore Solomon asks, "Who is as the wise man and what does it mean to be wise?"

To be wise means to operate in wisdom. So let's define "wisdom." Webster's Dictionary says that it is the quality of being wise, the power of judging rightly and following the soundest course of action based on knowledge, experience, understanding, etc.; good judgment capacity. In Strong's Exhaustive Concordance it is defined as "chokmak" which means, "in a good sense."

When we operate in wisdom, we are confident and therefore our face shines or beams. Why? We know we're making the right choice in a particular situation. That is why God says to seek out godly counsel before going ahead with your plans. You must have a good understanding of the situation.

In another passage of text it says, "If any man lacks wisdom, let him ask of God who gives liberally and upbraids not." God is saying that he has the answer to all of our questions and decisions. So, if you lack wisdom concerning what to do in a particular situation, ask God. He has promised that he will give you the answer liberally (generously) or freely in abundance, and not take it back. Be open to receive the answer in ways you may not expect and even from people you may not expect. God can use anyone and anything. So listen with an open heart to hear and see. God is speaking.

Also, he is looking for the person who will do His will, and live in peace through grace. Right thinking based on God's law of liberty, produces right thinking, which produces right believing, which produces right living.

In this chapter, the Word says to keep God's commands. It also talks about the importance of keeping the king's commandment, or in essence keeping the words of God, which are written in the Bible.

Keep the vows you make to God and keep the laws of the land; don't be in a hurry to go out and do evil or break the laws of the land. Why? Because God (and the king over you) does whatever he wills. He has power to do whatever he wills, and whatever he wants. He gives the command, which is immediately executed by his angels. If you do that which is good (just/honest) you will not experience the wrath of God, nor the king, but rather the good that comes along with it; however, if your doings are evil (unjust), beware. For, whatsoever a man sows that shall he also reap, and there is no respect of persons.

Romans 13:1-2 says, "Let every soul be subject to the governing authorities. For there is no authority, but of God. The powers or authorities that be, are ordained of God. Whosoever resists, resists what God has appointed and arranged in divine order, and those that resist will bring down damnation or hard judgment upon themselves (receiving the penalty due them). Therefore, we must be subject to God and the authorities of the land not only to avoid the wrath, but for conscience sake."

Additionally, Romans 13:6, 7 clearly states that we are under the command of God to pay taxes or tribute in the land in which we live. The authorities of the land are operating under God and are his servants. (If they are not operating righteously, he will deal with them.) Pay everyone you owe; pay taxes to whom taxes are due, and the same with regard to revenue, respect, and honor. Keep out of debt and don't owe anyone anything except to love them and keep God's commandments to love Him with all your heart, soul, mind, and strength, and love your neighbor as yourself." So whoever keeps the commandment will not feel the wrath of God.

You know, I have an older brother who taught me this lesson in a way in which I will never forget. When I became sick and fell into an unexpected hardship and needed a place to go and people to look out for me, he and his beautiful wife were among others who took me in and cared for me. In our conversations he would always say, "I am my brother's keeper." He said that his brother is anyone who needs his help, anyone God brings in his path. In the time I spent with them, they taught me more than I could ever learn from a multitude of textbooks.

If from your heart you will do what is right, God will tremendously bless you. It really is true; you receive back what you give out. Take time to listen to people, care about others, and be kind. It brings such a good feeling and inner reward.

You'll know just the right time to do what is necessary, for a wise man's heart discerns both time and judgment. What does it mean to discern? In the Hebrew language the word is transcribed "yada" which means to know (advise, answer, appoint, assuredly, be aware, observation, care, recognition, comprehend, be diligent, have understanding). This means that a wise man's heart (a man who operates in wisdom or good sense), or soul (his mind, will, and emotions) has the ability to know the exact time to take the necessary action. He never acts out of timing or in bad judgment or decisions. He clearly knows that every purpose has a correct time to happen and requires a correct decision to be made.

If you find that you are not acting as a wise man, your misery will be great because you won't know the correct timing or decisions to make in circumstances of life. This is why we must ask God everything, for no man knows what shall be on the earth or when it shall occur and for sure no one knows the exact time of his death. God has stated in Psalm 91 that the one who dwells in the secret place of the Most High God shall abide (live) under the shadow (protection) of the Almighty. He further states that because this man has set his love upon him, therefore, he will deliver him, and with long life he will satisfy him and show this man his salvation.

In chapter 8 of Ecclesiastes, it also says that no one can keep himself alive, only God can. As surely as man is born into the earth, so must he die and leave it. The writer says that there is no discharge in this war. (Just as a side note, I am thankful for the rapture or the catching away of the church.) The only people whose bodies shall not die or decay shall be those who in the last days are raptured or called out as in I Thessalonians 4:15-17It states, "For this we say unto you by the Word of the Lord, that we which are alive and remain unto the coming of the Lord shall not prevent them which are asleep (dead). For the Lord Himself shall descend from heaven with a shout, with the voice of the archangel, and with the trump of God: and the dead in Christ shall rise first. Then we which are alive and remain shall be caught up together with them in the clouds to meet the Lord in the air: and so shall we ever be with the Lord." Hallelujah, those who accept Jesus Christ as Lord and Savior of their lives, and who are here when He comes in the sky for his Body (the church), shall not taste death, but shall be caught away with Him.

So, except for those who are raptured by God in the last days, no one shall escape death; however, the righteous shall be raised to be with the Lord forever, but not so for the wicked. Their wickedness shall not deliver them. They shall die in their wickedness and enter judgment and eternal punishment.

In Revelation 20:11-15 we find this heart rending passage, "and I saw a great white throne and him that sat on it from whose face the earth and the heaven fled away; and there was found no place for them, and I saw the dead, both small and great stand before God: and the books were opened: and another book was opened, which is the book of life; and the dead were judged out of those things which were written in the books according to their works, and the sea gave up the dead which were in it; and death and hell delivered up the dead which were in them; and they were judged every man according to their works, and death and hell were cast into the lake of fire. This is the second death, and whosoever was not found written in the book of life, was cast into the lake of fire. Here it is very evident that there is no escape for the wicked!

After pondering all of this in his heart, the writer asks if you have ever watched people go to and fro, here and there in life? I have. At times I purposely set aside time to watch people. It's really interesting to observe people doing their daily routines. I love to study people and to understand what makes one person think and act a certain way in a situation and another person behave totally different. They have entirely different viewpoints. Why is this?

Solomon says that in his observations he has found that there is a time when one man rules over another and oppresses him. This wicked man doesn't even know that it is actually working to his own hurt. Why? God sees and observes all and he will reward accordingly.

The wicked man came, oppressed the people, and died (actually causing his own destruction in going against or oppressing the holy). After his death, no one remembers him. He is quickly forgotten. How terribly vain or empty this is. What did his life mean? He came and he went and no one cared!

Sometimes wicked people think that God's judgments will not come to them. They foolishly think that because they continue to do wickedly and there is seemingly not immediate punishment, they have gotten away with the evil. Therefore their hearts are bent on doing evil. What they have not considered is that God is fully aware of their evil hearts and deeds. What happens though is that man interprets God's long-suffering and mercy to mean that he will not judge and that no harm will come to them. But this is not so, for the wrath of God shall come upon the wicked and overtake him in his wickedness. The wicked shall not prolong his days, which are as a shadow (quickly passing away), because he doesn't fear God. It shall always go well with those who reverence (fear) God.

Even though there are injustices in the land, God will always deliver the righteous. Sometimes things have happened to the righteous that seemingly should be happening to the wicked, and then things to the wicked that seemingly should be reserved only for the righteous. He says that this is vain or empty (unexplainable). But never fail to remember righteous man that God says in Isaiah 54:17, "No weapon formed against you shall prosper, and every tongue that rises up against you in judgment, you shall condemn, for this is the heritage of the servants of the Lord, and their righteousness is of me, says the Lord." So, though it may look like things are reversed, they are not.

Solomon says that the best life is a life in God, but for a person without God he has nothing to look forward to. This life on earth is all he has. He will not be rewarded in the time to come. The righteous will rise again and live eternally with God in great joy and peace, but the unrighteous shall not, but shall live in everlasting torment. So, for him there is nothing better to do in this life on earth (if he will not accept God's free gift of life through His Son Jesus Christ,), and come under God's rule, but to eat, drink, and be merry as he toils through the days of his life that God has given him under the sun.

Even in all of this, there are also people who are so busy that it's hard for them to sleep day or night. They are always doing something. They try to fill each calendar day, every hour and minute, with busyness (business). Some are so busy until they don't take time for people and for life itself! Don't you know that life is about people and how we love and treat one another? Many of us have been known to live for tomorrow and not appreciate today, when in fact it's all about today, today! I don't mean you should not prepare for the future (that is absurd), but don't forget the people who you are interacting with today. Don't forget to be kind to those God places in your pathway each day, especially your family. Many times we are more kind to those outside of our families, but kindness begins at home. If you are this busy, you are too busy.

This reminds me of a time in my life that I'd over extended myself and was involved in multiple things at one time. Have you ever done this? Well, I was so busy that I'd forgotten to renew my auto registration in May and it was now August. Most likely I would have gone on thinking it was done, if it had not been for the police officer that pulled me over one day! Actually, when I saw the lights flashing and heard his siren, I kept going, because surely it wasn't for me. Seeing his persistence, I decided to stop. He said, "Miss when was the last time you had your vehicle registered?" I replied, "On my last birthday in May." And with a puzzled look on his face he replied, "Really?" Then he asked me to step outside the car and look at my tags. I gasped in surprise, Oh my goodness, it was the birthday the year before! He said, "Lady, anyone that busy is too busy!"

Yet in all of man's wisdom and all of this busyness there is not, never has been, and never shall be anyone as wise as God. When considering all of God's work, man cannot find it out! No one knows everything that has happened in the past, the works that were done under the sun; neither do any of us know what shall happen in the future. God reveals to man glimpses of events that he chooses to reveal and to whom he chooses to reveal them. Even with that, we don't know exactly when these events shall occur. "For we prophesy in part and we know in part." Even though a wise man studies and seeks out God's work, he will not be able to find it out. Only God is the all wise One! Only God knows the beginning, middle, and the end of a matter. Worship Him as the only true, wise God!

Food For Thought

1. What does wisdom mean to you?

2. Have you ever had a challenging area in your life? How did you handle it? Did you seek God 1st or try to figure it out?

3. Since wisdom is the practical application of knowledge, and God says to us what if any of us lacks knowledge, ask Him and he'll give it to us liberally.

   Why do we wait so long before asking? How will you handle future challenges?

4. Sometimes some of our decisions create more business for us. Our solutions can cause us excess work. God's ways are simple to follow. Is there an area that needs immediate attention in your life? Take a moment to ask God how to solve it. Afterward, write down the response. He may direct you to a passage of scripture, to an article in a magazine, prompt you to call someone, or just speak to you in your spirit. He's not limited.

5. Now act on what you heard. Don't wait. Why? Your head will reason against it, and you won't follow through on what you heard.

Chapter Nine

A NEW DAY!

Life is given to us by God to live with great enjoyment, happiness, and contentment.

Seeing that death is inevitable and happens to all and no man knows when it shall be, how should we live our lives? Purpose in your heart to enjoy each day, to be thankful for that day, and to be diligent in the task God has given to you. The author wrote that whatever your hands find to do, do it heartily, as unto the Lord God, for death comes to all-alike and no one can escape it. As a net is spread to catch its game, so also is death.

Determine not to be like a mere human being apart from God whose heart is deceitfully wicked and who lives his life devising and carrying out evil plans. Ecclesiastes says that madness (foolishness, folly, evil) is in his heart (his very being) while he lives! Death shall come to him and he shall be taken away in his evil.

While you are still alive, there is always "hope." If you are reading this right now, there is hope. You see, you still have breath in your body. It doesn't matter what the circumstances are that surround you, good or bad, favorable or unfavorable, there is still hope. The fact that you are breathing means there is "hope!" God had graciously given you this day to do good, love life, and to make a difference in this world! It is a gift.

You may have blown it yesterday or even five minutes ago, or five seconds ago; however, it all became your past. You now have a very unique window of time to make a difference, to effect a change. The question now is, "What will you do with this time?"

How will you live the rest of your life? Society doesn't have to be in your favor; other men and women don't have to be on your side. But God has promised and he cannot lie that if he is for you, who can be against you?

So now ask yourself, "What will you do with this day?" Solomon even says that a living dog is better than a dead lion. The dog sees, hears, tastes, smells, and feels his surroundings, but a dead lion neither notices nor recognizes them. He has lost all communication with this world; neither is he anymore a part of it. While he lived he was fierce, but dead he is nothing to be feared; no one is moved by his past roar.

Even if you are facing negative situations right now, death is never the answer, but rather life because if you are alive there is hope. Webster's dictionary says that hope is "a desire accompanied by expectation, and that it is a feeling that what is wanted will happen." If you take "hope" and join it hand-in-hand with "faith in God" and are diligent to do what he instructs in His Word, the thing that you believe God for (expect to happen) will happen!

DON'T EVER GIVE UP!!! Don't ever sell or trash your hope. Just keep living and doing what God has said and at the appointed time it will come to pass. I've noticed in God's Word it says many times, "at the appointed time, or in due time, or in the fullness of time." So give it "Time."

Live your life according to God's plans and purposes. Determine to enjoy each day with those whom he has placed around you. Love and laugh with them, fellowship and enjoy their company. Work at the job he has given you and be diligent to give it your very best. Show love, kindness, and mercy to all, especially your own family, for once you are dead; these things will be no more. In fact, all of the things you are angry or worried about now, all disappointments and concerns, strivings to become someone very important, your thoughts and opinions on a matter, your hopes, your fears, everything about you in this life will be over at an appointed moment that neither you nor those around you know.

I believe that Solomon said it best in verse seven of this chapter. "Go thy way, eat thy bread with joy, and drink thy wine with a merry heart; for God now accepts thy works. "Please let me bring clarity to this verse. It is not talking about eating gluttonously and getting drunk, but the rather to not worry about life, but enjoy and be thankful for the provision of God. Enjoy this life, enjoy this day; be merry (if you are in God's hands) for he has already accepted your work.

So, if you are married, then live a life of joy with your spouse; if you are not, then be joyful with those around you. Don't be picky or overly concerned with a matter. It won't matter when you are gone (dead). <u>Some things aren't even worth discussing</u>; deal with what is really important and forget the rest! Genuinely love as God loves and enjoy your life. Make the best of your appointed days. Live them joyfully!!!

Whatever your hand finds to do, do it with everything within you – go ahead and work, fulfill your dreams! For in the grave there is no work to be done, no more opportunities for you to express yourself or follow your dreams. What lifelong dream have you had? What is your "Someday" thing you will do or accomplish? Why are you still tucking it away and not acting upon it? What are you waiting for? Do not allow fear to grip you or doubt to hold you back one second longer. I heard a minister say that many people have been buried with unfulfilled, dreams in them. They never acted on them, and now it is too late. There are various fears that you must confront and press through.

Sometimes it is the fear of failure, fear of success, fear of being different (unaccepted), the fear of change that has kept people limited in their thinking and actions, and has held them back in life.   I encourage you to step out of your fear, doubt, unbelief, or even low opinion of yourself and dare to dream and accomplish your dreams!

Remember that the race of life isn't given to those who run it in hurry or the fastest, nor to those who are the strongest, neither is the provision to the wisest, or even riches to men of great understanding, nor favor to the skillful, but time and chance comes to us all. God has puts gifts in you to profit with and He expects fruit, (profit), from them.

While you live, take advantage of the times and opportunities that God sends your way. Don't allow it to be said that you died with unfulfilled dreams. Step out of the "boat of comfort" and do something; it's in you. God will help you. He is the God who teaches you to prosper and to get wealth that he may establish his covenant. Since you don't know the time of your death, do it now! Ecclesiastes 9:12 says that the sons of men are snared in an evil time when calamity falls upon them suddenly. In this passage, "sons of men" is referring to the "sons of Adam" (mankind), but we as believers in the Lord Jesus Christ, are no longer sons of men, but rather "sons of God." And His Holy Spirit within us guides us daily in the right paths. "Suddenly" means, "unexpectantly," or "not foreseen." So if you are in Christ <u>God has promised long life to us who dwell in his secret place and walk in his counsel.</u> Use it wisely.

I advise you to get God's wisdom in "every" situation of life and do what he says. He once told me to **see**, **hear**, **listen**, and **do**. See what he is saying, hear it clearly, listen (be very attentive), and then do it!

Solomon closes this chapter by telling us a story about a city that was going to be captured by a strong king. He built all types of bulwarks (strong holds) around it and prepared with his great army to overtake it in battle! No one could deliver this little city out of his great hands. No one was found strong enough.

However, a little old poor wise man lived in the city and by his wisdom (application of knowledge and understanding), the city was saved! How was this done? He gave wise counsel (thoughts) to the people in the government, and when they applied this, they were able to save the entire city! Hooray!

Unfortunately, even this little old poor, but wise man was not remembered after death. This though does not negate the fact that wisdom is better than strength. For strength was not able to save the city. His wisdom delivered them and words of wise men heard in quietness are better than the loudness of fools who rule!

Yes, wisdom is better than weapons of war, but one sinner can come along and destroy much good! Why? His thoughts are not God's, and therefore they are foolish.

When you consider that God knows everything and that all of the righteous man's works are in His hands, what type of person should you be? God sees all, hears all and knows all. He knows the plans he has for you; he already designed these plans. It's like when an architect designs a house. He draws a draft or blueprint of what he sees in his head. In the blueprint he will factor in every room, skillfully designing every dimension. Many times he already has a clear picture of even the type of furniture that would best suit the room and what functions it should be used for. God, in his infinite wisdom has already designed a Master Plan for us to follow.

If we follow it, then we will have good success. Joshua 1:8 says, "This book of the law shall not depart out of your mouth; but thou shall meditate therein day and night that thou mayest observe to do according to all that is written therein: for then thou shall make thy way prosperous, and then thou shall have good success."

Another translation says, "Make sure you obey the whole law my servant Moses gave you. Do not turn away from it to the right or the left. Then you will have success everywhere you go. Never stop reading this Scroll of the Law. Day and night you must think about what it says. Make sure you do everything that is written in it. Then things will go well with you. And you will have great success."

We know that Jesus Christ is the fulfillment of the Law and that He fulfilled it for us. He didn't come to do away with the law, but rather to fulfill it. Now we are no longer under the Law but under Grace. I'd rather have the good success God is talking about here, rather than the fruit or reward of my own works brought on by my own decisions and opinions. I am very thankful for the grace we've been given through Jesus Christ, for in him we've been made righteous, and now enter into the Kingdom of God by faith. Hallelujah, we are now under the rules of the Kingdom, which operates by love. This love is so amazing and powerful. Before Jesus ascended to heaven he left on record a new commandment in John 13:34, "A new commandment I give unto you, that you love one another as I have loved you, that you also love one another.

Food For Thought

1. **What will you do with this season of your life? It's up to you to make a difference.**

2. **List the 5 things you can do today to better yourself; Now list 5 things to better life for someone close to you.**

3. **Many times we hope for something to happen, but don't take the necessary steps to make it happen. What are you hoping for?**

4. Do you have faith to believe it can happen?

5. If not, then read scriptures on faith, meditate on them until it's in your spirit and belief system. Then act on your faith.

6. What steps will you need to take next to make your hope a reality?

7. When will you do this? (Give yourself a deadline).

8. You may need to get an accountability partner to assure that it gets done.

9. Do it now while there is time.

Chapter 10

<u>Prince or Pauper</u>

When a perfumer is making perfume, if dead flies get in it, it will be ruined and begin to stink! So it is with life! When a person who is known for wisdom does folly or foolishness, his folly then outweighs all the wisdom he was accredited with. Dead flies give off a foul odor that literally turns your stomach or makes it feel sick. It is so irritating to your nose! Pew! So is foolishness to him who is known for wisdom.

A wise man will be led by the Spirit of God; but a fool by his own wisdom or heart,. That's why this particular chapter in Ecclesiastes says that a wise man's heart turns him toward his right hand, but a fool's heart to his left hand. The right here symbolizes power and authority, and the left weakness of a man.

Even when a fool walks along the road of life, he is known as a fool because his decisions show him to be a fool. He is identified by his choices.

Wisdom shows that if a ruler rises up against you, don't resist him; silence your mouth, for gentleness stops a great offense. A fool would not think this way. He would utter all that is in his heart. However, know that not everyone in a high position or office operates in wisdom, some are foolish. The irony is that you have foolish people in high places, but wise people in low places. There are men that are slaves to things in this life like careers, positions, etc. that sit in high places, and yet there are princes who think they are slaves and live with a "slave" mentality. They have low self-esteem and a "less than" opinion of themselves.

Many times I observe people walking along the streets with a despair look on their faces, without any hope and downtrodden. My heart is so grieved for them because I know they are princes, God's wondrous creation, made in His glorious image. Yet, they are not aware of it, or have trouble receiving it. Our job as Christians is to tell them who they are, who God is, and who he has made them to be. We must convince them of the truth of God's Word and help them understand that Jesus, God's Son, gave his life as payment for their sins. He has redeemed them from the curse of the Law and made the way for them to walk in absolute victory and fulfillment as sons of the Living God!

It's the same in high places as in low. I have been in high places and talked with people who are in elevated positions and are weighed down with fear and gripped with pain. Their plastic smiles would seem to say, "I'm fine and in need of nothing." It only takes one moment of conversation to discover that they too are held in bondage to fears and pains, and need the redeeming power of God's unconditional love!

This world system designed by our enemy, satan, is filled with much animosity and greed. It breeds the mentality of get ahead by stepping on your neighbor, or digging a pit or trap. It says that in order for you to succeed you must degrade your fellowman. I've worked in the corporate world and have seen much of this happening on a regular basis. Things were done in greed to the hurt of the innocent and no one took it to heart! But know that he who digs a pit for others will himself fall into it. It may not come swiftly, but it will come! He who cheats will be hurt by his cheating; he who lies will be hurt by his lying.

In the book of Esther, God gives an account of a wicked prideful man named Hamon who had intense hatred for a Jewish man named Mordecai. His hatred was so deep that he not only wanted to have Mordecai killed, but his entire race annihilated. He even went so far as to get the king's approval and legally seal it. Everything was going according to his plans. He even built a gallows reaching 75 ft. high intending to hang Mordecai! But God discredited Hamon in the king's eyes, and the king ended up having Hamon hung on his own gallows! Mordecai was promoted to Hamon's position as 2nd in command to the king. The pit Hamon dug ended up being for him. Even his 10 sons that he bragged so much about were killed and hung up for all to see. Then all he had was given to Queen Esther and she put Mordecai over it. So, this passage is saying, don't do wickedly. Don't try to get ahead by stepping on your fellow man. Although others may not know, God, who sees and hears all, knows and He will repay! He is your shield and protector.

You may have to put forth more effort in doing what's right in order to excel, but God will see that you are promoted. Don't compromise your values and wisdom. It's not necessary for you to be a talebearer or a slanderer either to get ahead. Remember, a wise man <u>utters pleasant words</u> and <u>obtains much favor</u>. If a slanderer talks long enough he will show himself to be a fool. His continuous babbling is annoying! He is void of common sense. Doubly, if this man is a ruler, it's a sad thing. For he then is riotous in his living and has no morals and definitely no wisdom.

But blessed is the land (city, state, country, a nation) whose ruler is a noble honest man prone to wisdom and not riotous living. He's a man who is diligent and not slothful, who cannot be bribed with anything, especially money, promotion, or prestige.

This life has many valleys and mountain top experiences, but don't get so caught up in everything that you don't take time for laughter, dancing, and rejoicing. Know that there is a time for everything. Pace yourself, be balanced and flexible. A wise man knows when and how to rightly embrace each phase of life.

In this chapter it says, "Money answers all things." A wise man knows this means that since money is the form of trade we use to buy and sell, it is necessary, but not the principle thing. The principle thing is wisdom. You can have a lot of money but if you don't know the purpose of it and how to properly use it, it is to no avail. What makes you a man wise in this area is that you are not foolish enough to worship it, but rather you worship God who gives the money. A fool will worship the money because he is void of understanding and does not know or take to heart that money is only his servant, put here to serve him. So, he winds up serving that which was meant to serve him. The money is God's and we are caretakers of it. How beautiful when it is used for the furtherance of His Kingdom, and how He directs. "The earth is the Lord's and the fullness thereof, the world, and they that dwell therein." (Psalm 24:1, I Cor. 10:26).

Finally, we are counseled to "speak well of our dignitaries." Curse them not, not even in our thoughts. Well that's a big one! How many times do we hear people speaking evil of our dignitaries? God didn't say to speak well only when they are doing right, but speak well of them. He'll take care of what he needs to take care of. You are divinely placed in your land for God's purposes. Pray for your leaders that they will be men and women of honesty and integrity. Pray for their salvation, after all, they are the leadership of your land. When the righteous rule the people rejoice.

Study Questions

1. **Think of an instance where you were led by God's wisdom. Now think of one that was your wisdom. Compare the two: What was the difference in the outcomes? How much simpler was God's than yours? God will always give wisdom to whoever asks.**

2. **Have you ever been confronted by a foolish person who made an unfounded accusation against you? Did you defend yourself? If so, did it work? Not usually. Using the information in this chapter, what is the best way to handle this situation?**

3. **It's evident from reading chapter 10 of Ecclesiastes that God not only wants us to be wise and behave ourselves wisely in this world, but He also desires for us to be happy. He gives us balance in all things.**

4. Get a 1 month calendar and pencil in days that you will do something fun, then stick to it. Clear your calendar of all the serious things on those days. Laughter does good like a medicine. It really does!

Chapter 11

SOWING AND REAPING PRINCIPLES

Chapter eleven of Ecclesiastes deals with some very important subjects, such as wisdom and guidance for the youth, and God's principles concerning money, i.e. sowing and reaping. I have discovered that God has much to say in the Bible about money.

God gives us the key to giving and receiving. It's in the letting go or releasing of what we have in our hands, and the giving to others. Look at Matthew 6:3-4, "But when thou doest alms (giving) let not thy left hand know what thy right hand doeth. That thine alms may be in secret, and thy Father which seeth in secret himself shall reward thee openly." Luke 6:38 piggybacks this by saying, "Give and it shall be given unto you; good measure, pressed down, shaken together, and running over, shall men give into your bosom. For with the same measure that ye mete (give out) withal it shall be measured to you again."

The Amplified Bible puts it this way, "Give and (gifts) shall be given to you; good measure, pressed down, shaken together, and running over will they pour into the pouch formed by the bosom of your robe and used as a bag. For with the measure you deal out with the measure you use when you confer benefits on others, it will be measured back to you."

God once illustrated to me the power of a seed. Once it was planted in the earth, it exploded underneath the ground, ripping throw the soil at an astronomical speed, multiplying itself as it went along! Then in sprouted above ground, and within time it grew to a tremendously fruitful vine! One seed sown in good soil has unlimited returns.

Go ahead, cast or throw like a football, your bread or substance (money) upon the waters (or areas where there are people who need it). After many days, or in time, it will return to you in good measure. Whenever you have the opportunity to give, do it liberally and with joy, not stingily, for you never know what the future holds for you; you may someday have a need. Life is unpredictable and full of many surprises! Only God knows what is ahead even to the smallest detail. Some seasons bring sunshine and others bring rain. The sunshine means good times and the rain means the tough or harder times. If we knew ahead of time that we were entering a rainy season, we'd prepare by putting on our rain gear. However, we do not know, but God does and he wants us to trust in Him.

I'm sure you can relate to times in your life when you experienced great losses or disappointments. We are never quite prepared for them (the rainfalls). I am so thankful that God always has people there to help us get through these times and others walk with us into the sunny seasons. If during the time of your sunny season you are sowing and giving cheerfully, then your provision will be there for the seasons of torrential rains (adversity).

I was sitting at a funeral waiting for others to arrive, when a young woman sat beside me. After quite a while of stillness, she asked me whether I used to attend a church in another state. I said yes, I used to be an associate pastor there. Then she said, "I thought it was you. I remember you!" She asked if on occasion I'd ever given anyone money during a church service. I said, "Yes, when God told me." She then proceeded to tell me about the first time she had visited the church. She had just moved to the location and was going through some rough times (rainy season). She said that there was a lady there who gave her money and said it was from the Lord. Well, it took a while, but then I remembered her face and the day God spoke to me to give her the money from Him. I was so happy that God had used me to help someone in need. Only God knew her exact need.

Years later, I found myself having an area of need (walking through a rainy season) and God sent people to sow into my harvest field. I wonder what would have happened if I had held on tightly to what I had (for fear of not getting anymore), and not given to that lady? I believe I would have stopped my own increase or jammed up my water well.

If you look at your own condition and try to figure out if you can give, you'll never do it. Since I was a widow, in the natural it would have appeared that I couldn't give to her and still have what I needed. (That's observing the wind or regarding the clouds to determine if you can give.) Anything that prohibits you from doing what God speaks to you to do, and what you know in your heart you should do, is regarding the clouds or circumstances.

Finally, we do not know the way of the spirit, nor how the bones of a child grow in the mother's womb; so ideally, we do not know the works of God who makes it all. So in the morning sow your seed (like a farmer) and in the evening sow (plant) your seed, for you do not know which of these will prosper, or if perhaps both will. So when the conditions are good and when they're not so favorable, put your trust in God. He will take good care of you.

Ecclesiastes is saying, "I trust you will have many pleasant, sun shining days and seasons in your life, but know that days of darkness or torrential rains are also coming. It's all a part of life. Sow that you may have the joy of giving, and that you and your family may reap in the days ahead!"

Now let's deal with wise instruction to the young. Young person, operate in God's wisdom early. Go ahead and rejoice when you are young, enjoy your youth and let your heart bring you much happiness. Walk in the ways of your heart (in God) and in the sight of your eyes, but use wisdom, for God will bring you into judgment (his justice) for all of these things. If you walk in integrity, you'll receive good now and in the days to come, but, if in dishonesty you'll receive the judgment due the evil. It is possible to have good clean fun and to enjoy your youthful days. God has designed them just for you.

Stay clear of foolishness and remove the lusts from your heart, (the lust of the eyes, lust of the flesh, and the pride of life), for they will only lead to sorrow and the torments of your mind. In a time when you should be free of care, you will find yourself burning inside with lusts (unsatisfied desires). Be kind, considerate, compassionate, and loving. Seek to know God and follow his ways. Be thankful and grateful unto your parents and those in authority. Honor God and don't speak evil of dignitaries. Respect the elderly, considering that you too shall someday walk in their shoes (if you live wisely and not foolishly).

Take to heart that your days of youth are fleeting. They're passing quickly! You will not always be a child or youth. Time has a way of escaping from our catch. Years can pass by without our knowing it, and then we who were youth yesterday are now adults today. He who is a young adult today, will be an elderly person tomorrow, and he who was elderly today, shall tomorrow be on earth no more. In light of this, it behooves us to make wise choices and decisions in this life, knowing that for them you shall give an account to God.

Again, I must interject, thank God for grace! If you are in Christ, you are a new creation. Old things have passed away! Behold, **all** things have become new. As Christ is, so are we in this earth. Bless God, when He looks at us He sees Christ's righteousness. I'm so glad that He does, aren't you?

Food For Thought

1. List your thoughts about money.

2. List your understanding of stewardship. What is a steward?

3. Everything belongs to God Almighty and we steward it. If as a steward you are taking care of what belongs to someone else, how should you treat that property or item.

4. Who owns the stuff you or the owner?

5. If the owner owns it, then He has the right to direct how it is to be used and when it is to be given, right?

6. Can God trust you with what is His?

7. Can He trust you to implement his plan exactly as He lays it out?

7. If He can, he will continue to give you, so you can give to others.

8. Considering the span of our lifetime and the compression of the days, what choices will you make today to affect your tomorrow? Tomorrow comes very quickly.

Chapter 12

<u>At the End of the Day</u>

What, know you not that your body is the temple of the Holy Spirit, and that Christ has purchased it with His own blood?

Let's explore the last chapter of this tremendously wise book and find out what Ecclesiastes has to say about the body? Well, for one, the Holy Spirit is speaking through King Solomon admonishing the young people to remember their Creator, God Almighty, in the days of their youth, while they are vibrant and strong, full of energy! Why? The years have taught King Solomon that soon night comes. Almost seemingly before you know it, you have entered your twilight years, years of the finalization of the aging process.

He says, "So give God your youth before your eyes grow dim, (when the muscles behind the eyes grow weak and lose their elasticity) or dimness of sight, before the hearing ear no longer hears the pleasant voices around it, and yes, even when the birds' chirping is annoying. It robs you of the little sleep you do get. Before the keepers of the house, (or the nervous system), shall tremble, the knees become feeble, and the grinders for teeth cease or are so few that eating is a chore!

Yes, many times the aging process brings with it some uninvited friends, not people but ailments and other unwanted obstacles. For instance, some have experienced fear of height, definitely shying away from climbing high buildings, riding amusement rides, and all the daring things that young people live for! The writer in his kindness refers to the flourishing of the almond tree, which is a nice terminology for gray hair covering the land! Try as we might, the dyes only last for a season, and even during the season, the gray continues to peak out as a gentle reminder us that our bodies are growing older!

Amazingly enough, even the little issues can seem big at this time in life; a grasshopper shall be a burden. Even the desire shall fail! Sometimes it's been the desire for life's excitement and the sexual desire, as hormones diminish and the testosterone level decreases.

I've noticed that toward the end of a man's life, his appetite begins to wane and food is no longer desirable. It's as if the body's craving or desire for appetizing food is suddenly cut off.

Remember God in your youth! Serve him with excitement and great joy while you are young, before all of this takes place and the very chords of life themselves are broken, (the bloodstream and blood vessels). Do this before the wheel of life, is broken at the cistern, (or spine), because (the body) will then return to the earth from which it was made, and the spirit of the man will return to God, the Creator who gave us breath in our bodies.

In light of all of this, consider the type of person you should be. That's why Romans 12 says for us to present our bodies a living sacrifice, holy and acceptable unto God (our Creator), which is our reasonable service. How do we do this? We do this by not conforming to this world's ways and thoughts, but rather being transformed by the renewing of our minds.

Do you remember the transformer toys? They look like one character and then after a few twists and turns, amazingly they become something else. When we present our bodies as a living sacrifice, holy and acceptable to God, we will prove what is that good and acceptable will of God in Christ Jesus concerning us.

The writer could have said as a sacrifice, but instead he said, "Living." When our bodies are living, they are alive. It's like saying, "While there is life still in them, give them to God as a sacrifice, not a gift but a sacrifice. The Greek word for sacrifice is "thusia" which is derived from "thuo" which means sacrifice, to immolate, slaughter for any purpose, kill or slay. We know we are not to literally kill our bodies (God is life), but we are to kill those fleshly desires that go against God's Word.

It almost seems like an oxymoron in saying to present our bodies as a living "sacrifice" when we know that they are usually slain. How can we do this and still live? How can we be alive yet slain? Easy! The portion that is alive is our physical breathing body, yet the portion that is slain is our soul or fleshly desires and appetites for this world system and the things of the world. Galatians 5:19-21 details the many works of the flesh.

We choose to die to the conformity of this world system and through applying the Word of God to our lives daily; we are continually transformed into Christ's image. As we renew our minds with His Holy Word, we are changed. Galatians 5:22-26 gives us a list of the fruit of the Holy Spirit.

It is then imperative as young people, or at a very early age to embrace Christ and the Kingdom of God, which is righteousness, peace, and joy in the Holy Ghost.

In contrast, the world's system operates by the lust of the flesh, the lust of the eyes, and the pride of life. It is by these three things that the first man and woman, Adam and Eve, fell from God's glory and into the slavery of sin. They lost their glory, the very Glory of God, which they once had! This then opened the door to the decaying process of their bodies and every person born thereafter. Why? Sin entered in and produced death.

God's word says that His people are destroyed for lack of knowledge. Destroyed in the Greek is "damah" or to be dumb or silent, or to fail, perish, cease, be cut down or off, be brought to silence, be utterly undone. Whereas the Greek word for lack is "bliy" which means failure, nothing or destruction. (God says in his word that where no vision is the people perish.).

Knowledge in the Greek is "death" or cunning, know, aware (wittingly), and is derived from another Greek word "yada" which has various meanings, some of which are, "to know, observation, care, recognition, instruction, designation, punishment, acknowledge, acquaintance (acquainted with), advise, answer, appoint, be aware, for a certainty, comprehend, consider, cunning, declare, be diligent, cause to discern, discover, endued with, familiar friend, instruct, cause to know, perceive, regard, skillful, teach, have understanding.

To sum it all up, if in our youth we do not receive the proper instruction, wisdom or knowledge from God's Word on a daily basis, there is a lack and this lack ultimately sets us up for destruction through the entrance of lust of the flesh, lust of the eyes, and the pride of life. That's why God is saying to remember him in your youth, while you're still young and tender, before life has had an opportunity to harden you.

Why also would God say to "remember" him instead of saying "consider" him? The words remember and consider both deal with our intellect but have distinctly different meanings. Webster's dictionary says, "Consider" means to look at carefully, examine, to think about it in order to understand or decide, to keep in mind, take into account, be thoughtful of.

"Remember" in the Hebrew language is "zakar" which means to mark (so as to be recognized), to mention, be mindful, recount, record, bring (call, come, keep, put) in remembrance, x still, think on, x well.

God is saying that rather than just looking carefully at him or examining him in order to try and understand him, spend time getting to recognize or know him. Make mention of him, be mindful of him, read what's written or recorded about him, and constantly think on Him in the days of your youth (each day). Then you will have good success and be able to make the right decisions, or take the right actions, and make your way prosperous.

If you say, "My youth has already been spent! Where was the book when I was growing up?" Well, we can't go back and regain the past; we can't as adults relive our youthful years, but we can move forward! A marching army is always better than a still one and a flowing stream better than a stagnant one! As long as there is breath in your body, there is opportunity to excel in the things of God. He is a restorer of the breach. Joel 2:28 says,

"I will restore to you the years the cankerworm has eaten, (the years that were eaten or destroyed). Aren't you glad that Almighty God can do this? With God nothing is impossible!!! We MUST do as the Apostle Paul said, "Forgetting those things which are behind and reaching forward toward the mark for the prize of the high calling of God which is in Christ Jesus. Phil. 4:13-14.

If you are still in your youth, take heed to wisdom and avoid the pitfalls of the enemy. When it's all said and done, many experiences in life are simply vanity, or vain and empty experiences without Christ. You don't need to experience everything. It's best to leave those chains of bondage where they are.

Man without the direction of God seems to have a "look at me perform" attitude, "I can do this better than you." There's a constant competing one against another. This is all vanity, for neither considers that each one has his own gifts, talents, and abilities from God, the Creator, for specific purposes. Once you understand this, you will never compete with anyone again for "center stage."

Give everything you are back to God and let Him show you who you are and why you are here (your purpose). Get to know him and take the necessary steps of obedience daily to bring to pass his will for your life. Develop a love relationship with him and stay there in His presence. Each day will draw you closer to Him.

As we conclude, we see that the writer said that he continuously sought out words to bring wisdom and knowledge to the people. I find that in an attempt to bring clear concise understanding to the people I teach, I seek out multiple ways of bringing knowledge, referencing and cross referencing material in order to present enough accurate information. Why do I go to such great lengths? I recognize, like King Solomon, that the words of the wise are as nails, which fasten down an area.

For instance, in building a house you must use the right nails. There's a nail that you use on the roof and a different nail for the basement. A wise builder knows what words (nails) to use. His wisdom comes from the Shepherd above, who alone has all the answers. The Bible actually has the answer to any question you might ask!

One thing about wisdom is that it is plenteous. There's no shortage! There's no end to the amount of books that can be written by man, and quite frankly, much studying can wear you out at times! The more we study and learn, the more books we write.

However, the Bible is the only book written by God Himself. All of our books are not to be compared in any way to it. It's like comparing the difference between the cone and the ice cream. Of course the feature is the ice cream; the cone only supports the ice cream. The ice cream makes the cone!

Food For Thought

1. **What things do you still have to do before His return? List them.**

2. **Who do you still need to witness to about salvation?**

3. What things or relationships might you need to change in your life to assure that you finish your purpose and destiny?

4. God gave you a purpose. He has set everything you need within reach, and everyone here to help you fulfill it. Do it now.

*   The book of Ecclesiastes was written thousands of years ago, however the writer was saying that time goes quickly! Today we see it whisking past us at a tremendous speed. Have you noticed that days and months are flying by! Truly the Lord Jesus is soon to come back.

Chapter 13

<u>The Conclusion</u>

Well let's quickly hear the conclusion of the whole matter. **If after living my entire life I had an opportunity to express final words, what would they be?** Have you noticed that at someone's death, he normally, if given the chance, sums up his whole life in very few words?

King David is recorded in II Samuel 23:1-4 as saying, "Now these are the last words of David. David, the son of Jesse said, and the man who was raised up on high, the anointed of the God of Jacob and the sweet psalmist of Israel said, The Spirit of the Lord spake by me, and his word was in my tongue."

"The God of Israel said, the Rock of Israel spake to me: He that ruleth over men must be just, ruling in the fear of God. And he shall be as the light of morning when the sun riseth, even a morning without clouds: as the tender grass springing out of the earth by clear shining after rain." Here the king is conveying his heartfelt belief about ruling.

On the same note, the Apostle Paul when nearing death sent a letter to Timothy, his son in the ministry. He said, "I charge thee therefore before God, and the Lord Jesus Christ, who shall judge the quick (living) and the dead at his appearing and his kingdom; preach the word: be instant in season, out of season; reprove, rebuke, exhort with all longsuffering and doctrine. For the time will come when they will not endure sound doctrine; but after their own lusts shall they heap to themselves teachers, having itching ears (who will tell them what they want to hear); and they shall turn away their eyes from the truth (because they don't want to hear sound doctrinal truth and correction), and shall be turned unto fables.

But watch thou in all things, endure affliction, do the work of an evangelist, make full proof of thy ministry (fully perform all your duties).

For I am now ready to be offered, and the time of my departure is at hand. (The time of my spirit's release from the body is at hand.) I have fought a good fight (of faith), I have finished my course, I have kept the faith: henceforth there is laid up for me a crown of righteousness which the Lord, the righteous judge, shall give me at that day, and not to me only but to all them that love his appearing (Jesus Christ's return)."

Even our Lord, Jesus as he neared the time of his betrayal by Judas in the Garden of Gethsemane said to his disciples, "Watch and pray, that ye enter not into temptation: the spirit indeed is willing, but the flesh is weak."

Luke 22 records the Passover Meal or Last Supper of Christ. In verse 15 Jesus, speaking to his disciples said, "With desire I have desired to eat this Passover with you before I suffer: for I say unto you, I will not anymore eat thereof until it be fulfilled in the Kingdom of God." This is where he took the bread, (his body), and the wine, (his blood), and communed with his disciples. He let them know that he was getting ready to offer himself to God as the Sacrificial Lamb without blemish, for the sins of all mankind.

He made a new covenant with God for man forever, the covenant in His blood, thus taking away all our sins, and giving us His righteousness.

He is like the lover in the Song of Solomon, who is so overwhelmingly in love with his bride to be. In accordance, this meal symbolizes his great love for us and desire to always be with us. Therefore, Jesus admonishes us to take communion often in remembrance of Him.

Have you ever had the rewarding experience of sitting with a friend before they die, before their spirit leaves their body? (I like to call it moving to another location.) If they are Christians, it's quite an eye opener! Forgive me, but I must take this moment to reminisce about past friends and loved ones who have made the transition. Their last words before embarking upon this journey are valued nuggets of love!

I call to remembrance my good friend, Valeria Chisolm! I remember distinctly our last day together. We laughed and talked about the goodness of God! I can still see the glistening in her eyes as I placed on her wrist the beautiful bracelet I'd brought back from Israel. I believe it was a gift from God to her. She was sick and could not have made the trip that far. Even in the midst of the illness, we could still always talk "girl talk."

That day, as the bracelet was placed on her wrist, something wonderful happened! She received new strength and we started figuring out what outfit looked good with that bracelet! We thought about the fact that a woman "always" needs a nice piece of jewelry! We began laughing and falling backwards on the bed in hysteria. In fact, we made so much noise until her husband came running upstairs to see what going on. He too joined in the laughter! She talked that day about her great love for the Master!

And how could I ever forget the transitioning of my own dear sweet "Granny" as she prepared for her journey. Granny has always been so very special to me! I used to hang under her almost everywhere she'd go. She was always in church singing about the goodness of the Lord. People called her Ms. Mabel, Aunt Mabel, Ms. Reed, or singing Evangelist Mabel Reed, but I affectionately called her Granny. This is the lady that let me play dress up in her jewelry, scolded and fed me, and helped to instruct me in the things of God. Her life molded my character in many ways. In her final hours here, although her voice could no longer be heard, her eyes still spoke of her breath taking love for God.

Through the years Granny taught me so much about loving my Creator and now in her death, I saw the culmination of that love. As our family and friends gathered around her beside to say "We'll see you later," and sing her into Glory, something truly unforgettable and amazing took place! We watched as her grayish aging eyes began to sparkle and change colors, turning the most beautiful shade of pale blue! The bluer they became, the more clearly we saw God's glorious reflection. The presence of Almighty God shown through them, piercing the souls of all who watched! Then in a moment, we knew Jesus had just come to meet her!

Yes, young people, I can assure you that God is real! Please love and serve him in the strength of your youth!

Permit me now to ask you a question. "What will your last words be?" Will you come to know the Creator, the Master and be able to leave wise instructions for others who have yet to complete this journey, or will you find yourself lost for words or expressions?

King Solomon, the wisest man to ever live, says, "Let us hear the conclusion of the whole matter:

1. Fear God, and

2. Keep his commandments:

For this is the whole duty of man. (The word "duty" in Hebrew is "dabar" which means commandment, portion, and purpose.) For God shall bring every work into judgment with every secret thing, whether it is good or whether it is evil." Luke 12:2 says, "For there is nothing (not even one thing) covered that shall not be revealed: neither hid that shall not be known."

All those who do not accept Jesus as their Lord and Savior must appear before the Judgment Seat of God at the Great White Throne Judgment. There you will face the Almighty God in the nakedness of your sins. Why not accept him now, and receive his love, grace and mercy. In fact, God our Father has his arms open wide waiting for you to come to Him. Let him love you. **Don't worry about what you've done wrong, or**

what people say, Jesus will wash you with his precious blood, and make you clean. In fact, God, the angels, and the host of souls in heaven are waiting to rejoice over you. In short, there's a party waiting there in your honor. Will you accept the invitation?

Take this moment to acknowledge him as God, and pray this salvation prayer with your mouth, from your heart. "Dear God, I thank you that you love me and that you gave your only Begotten Son, Jesus Christ, to die for my sins and to cleanse me from all unrighteousness. I am sorry for my sins; I accept your forgiveness and love. Jesus I believe that you are the Son of God, that you died for me, and that you rose again, and are now seated at the right hand of God, the Father, interceding on my behalf. Please come into my heart forever. Thank you, Jesus for your love. Thank you Lord. Now I confess that Jesus Christ, you are Lord of my life and my Savior.

If you have accepted the Lord Jesus Christ as our Lord and Savior, his blood has paid for our sins, washed our slate clean and gained us entrance into God's Kingdom as His sons. It's a brand new day! If any man be in Christ he is a new creation, old things are passed away, behind (listen!) All things have become new! Hallelujah, our names are written in the Lamb's Book of Life!

I pray that if you have not made a decision to accept Jesus as your Lord and Savior you will do so now. God is love and he loves you so very much. He gave his most precious gift, (he could give no greater gift)! He gave his only begotten Son, Jesus Christ for you.

The Bible says that the soul that sins must surely die. This would be you and me, for all have sinned and come short of the glory of God. However, Jesus came and died in our place, shedding his righteous blood for our sins. He took on death and gave us life, thus securing our eternal salvation. Just pray the salvation prayer from your heart and your name will be written in the Lambs Book of Life. Receive God's love which surpasses anything you've ever imagined! Continue to live in reverence and honor of God by loving Him and loving others as Jesus Christ has loved you. Keep your eyes on Christ, and soon He will return. "Keep Looking Up!"

Study Help Questions

1. **What words of wisdom can you leave the next generation?**

2. **What could you do today, in this season of your life, to make the rest of your time here better for you?**

3. What could you do today, to make the rest of your time here better for someone else?

4. Who needs to know that you love them? Who needs to know you care?

5. What gifts, talents, and abilities do you have within you that can better this world? List them now and use them.

- Have you ever watched a good movie and as it neared the end, you wanted to prolong it? You just didn't want it to end. So is this life. It has a beginning, a middle (plot), and an ending.

- In this chapter, we've looked at some well known people and their last words to others. Basically, they summed up life's most important lessons in a few sentences. What life changing words could you share?

APPENDIX A

PRIDE

After thousands of years, God sent Jesus, His only begotten Son, to earth in the form of a newborn baby for the purpose of growing up to be a young man, and then offered as the "Final" and "Only" true sacrifice for mankind's sins.

"The Word of God became flesh and dwelt (lived) among us and we beheld his glory, as of the glory of the only begotten Son of God." It amazes me, and yet blesses me that God before the world began had already preordained a day and time for Jesus to be sacrificed as our Passover Lamb. In this I see the precious grace of the Almighty God. Now, through Jesus' Blood our sins are forever removed (not covered, but removed)! All we need do is turn to him, repent, and receive forgiveness and restoration. What an Awesome God!

"For this reason was the Son of God manifested, to destroy (totally annihilate) the works of the evil one." What are the evil ones works?

- The pride of life

- The lust of the flesh

- The lust of the eyes

All of these things come in the form of idolatry. Idolatry is anything that takes you away from your natural place in God where you reverence and honor Him as Lord. He should have a special seat in your heart and be of the highest esteem, a place reserved only for him. In fact, God is to be number one in your life. Anything that takes his place is illegal and a form of treason.

You may ask, "How do I know if I've made anything (anyone) an idol?" Well, that's an easy question. Whatever you think about first thing in the morning and last thing at night, whatever preoccupies your thoughts on a constant, daily basis instead of God is more than likely and idol. Is it money, things, people, prestige, fame, a business, etc.? Take an inventory of your thoughts and if you find an idol, just do housecleaning. Get into God's presence and repent. Repent means simply to change your thoughts, and thereby you will change your actions. He is faithful and just to forgive us of our sins and to cleanse us from all unrighteousness.

Remember, instead of trying to be a powerful or well-known individual, just be a true worshipper of God and love the brethren. God will bring you into your destiny. Each day will be a part of it, and everyday a new adventure will unfold.

These two commandments Jesus left for us, letting us know that all of the commandments are summed up into these two:

- Love the Lord your God with all your heart, all your soul, and all your mind and strength.

- Love one another as I have loved you.

Let's talk a little about "pride" since that is the area that the devil works so hard to deceive us with. Think about it? Satan tricked Judas through his "pride" and his **love of money**, which is the root of **all** evil. Think of a root of a plant or tree. The root is the area where all nourishment flows through. It actually is the means by which the plant or tree is fed. Judas' pride (root) actually created a door of access for greed to enter. All the enemy need is to get a toe in your life and then he comes in with both feet.

Full tree represents Judas Iscariot's life.

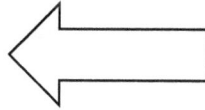

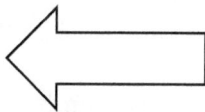

Satan entered in through the roots to get to Judas' heart. Love of money is the root of all evil. These were the roots in Judas' life.

If we will walk before our God as the other eleven disciples did we will not become filled with pride. How did they walk? They walked in humility, (humble) and reverence unto

God. Pride on the other hand produces high-mindedness, headiness/haughty, and what can be termed, "the big head!" Remember, it's Christ who does the work through you, so there's no need for the big head. Many times man can praise you and if you are not watchful you'll begin to think it's you. However, if you remain in humility through a relationship with God by prayer and reading His Word, you'll be able to give the praise and glory to God, knowing that it is He who does it all.

I love Philippians 2:6 which says, though Jesus was a son he thought it not robbery to be equal with God, but made of himself no reputation, he humbled himself (even to the death on the cross). If Jesus, who was the Son of God, gave all glory and honor to God, shouldn't we also.

Jesus was our "Passover Lamb." What exactly is a Passover Lamb? When the Israelites (God's chosen people) were in Egypt in captivity, on the night God was going to set them free, he instructed them to take an unblemished lamb, kill it, take the blood and smear it on the top of the door and doorposts of their houses. When the death angel (whom God sent to kill the first born of every household of the Egyptians) saw the blood, he would "pass over" their households and all in the house would live. Everyone had to be in the houses where the blood was smeared in order to receive protection.

This blood of these lambs covered the sins, but never removed sin. Jesus' Blood, however, is not like any other blood, in that it totally removed our sin instead of covering it up. Additionally, his blood brought healing and deliverance from all the work of the evil one. The word salvation in the Greek is "sozo," which means, salvation, healing, deliverance and prosperity. The Apostle Paul even recognized that all honor belongs to God for everything. He said, "I glory not except in the cross of Christ." Pride in contrast would say that you deserve the glory, but wisdom lets you know that it all belongs to God. We are his workmanship, created in Christ Jesus unto good works that he has before ordained that we should walk in them. (Eph. 2:10)

So now, if you're ever tempted to become prideful in any area, remember this catchy phrase, "The big-head is dead!"

Praising God keeps us surrendering ourselves under his will and gives honor and recognition to him as the Most High God. When we have this heart attitude, God **promotes** us. If God were to give us a place of position with people and his power (anointing), without us having the love of God as our "root," we'd become prideful just like satan and Judas and thus be positioned as enemies of God.

Question: Why does the world strive for position, people and power?
Answer: Satan is the ruler or prince of this present world system and it has taken on his character and adopted his concepts and beliefs. Adam's fall to sin through Satan's deception in the Garden of Eden brought every man (person) born hereafter under the rule of Satan whose kingdom operates on a lust or desire for:

1. **Position**

2. **People**

3. **Power**

4. **PRIDE**

His kingdom consists of:

1. **The lust of the flesh**

2. **The lust of the eyes**

3. **The pride of life.**

So, since lust is the basis for his kingdom rule, let's take a vivid look at "lust." According to Nelson's New Bible Illustrated Dictionary, lust is the desire for what is forbidden; an obsessive sexual craving; a desire for things that are contrary to the will of God (the lust after evil things). In I Corinthians Chapter 10 God shows us an example of the Israelite people in the desert, being overtaken in these lusts. Their lusts took their hearts so far away from God until they were filled with unbelief, and caused them to miss entering the Promised Land.

Christians are able to resist lust through the Power of the Holy Spirit who lives within us. The flesh (fleshly desires) with its passions and lusts is to be crucified as stated in Galatians 5:24 "And those who belong to Christ Jesus have crucified the flesh (the godless human nature) with its passions and appetites and desires," and also in Titus 2:11-12, "For the grace of God has come forward (appeared) for the deliverance from sin and the eternal salvation for all mankind. It has trained us to reject and renounce all ungodliness and worldly passions (desires), to live discreet (self controlled), upright devout (spiritually whole) lives in this present world.

Praise God that Jesus, the second Adam, (the spiritual Adam who was 100% God and 100% man), through his crucifixion and resurrection liberated us from satan's rule and brought us into the freedom of God's Kingdom. Through the offering of his precious holy Blood he paid the price for our sin and transgression, for the Bible states that the soul that sins must surely die, and that cursed is every man who hangs on a tree. Through his love for you and me, he willingly went to the Golgotha Hill carrying his wooden cross (made from a tree), and was nailed to it (hung on a tree), to liberate us from Satan's rule. Hallelujah for Jesus Christ, the Son of the Living God, Amen!

A fruit of lust is manipulation. You begin to manipulate people to get what you lusted over, whether it's something you've seen with your eyes, your flesh desires, or for position or money. (The love of money is the root of all evil.)

With manipulation comes control. There is a desire to "control" the circumstances or the people, or the money. Judas was only assigned to hold the money, but perhaps he wanted control over it, wanting to take ownership of what wasn't his. Judas was not the one in authority, Jesus was. He obviously was disregarding Jesus' authority because his heart was prideful. This showed that he felt he was equal in authority with Jesus! His love of money led him to betray the Son of God for thirty pieces of silver. .

The Bible says, "Either make the tree good or make the tree evil."

All trees have roots. A good tree's root is "Love." An evil tree's root is "the Love of Money" which is the root of all evil.

Pride was the one thing that took satan down from being an archangel in heaven. He had:

1. **Position**

2. **Authority (one of three arch angels)**

3. **Privilege (through worship as the "worship leader in heaven")**

He was found to be full of pride (he was lifted up in pride), and therefore lost his place in heaven at the throne of God Almighty. He desired in his heart to have God's position. Even though he was already high in rank but wanted to be the highest (pride). Pride will cause you to want to be better than everyone else!

Note: All of my growing up life I strove to be the best at everything, always better than everyone else at a thing. That's Pride. After the Holy Spirit opened my eyes to see this, I prayed to God to free me from this pride. He began to let me see areas in my life where pride had embedded itself, even hidden places. I had no idea it was there.

I always tried to be "perfect in everything." However, in striving to be perfect, I found that I was actually very self-centered. Even though I'd say it was about others, it always came back to "me." This is also a form of pride. For instance, why did I want others to do well? I'd say it was so I could see them doing good and excelling. Well, actually I would get a good feeling about the fact that I was able to help them do well. It always came down to the word "I." The "I" syndrome is at the base of every prideful thought, decision, and action.

What a relief to know that I don't have to be perfect; I'm already what God created me to be. I'm already complete in Christ Jesus. God is perfect; there is no flaw in Him! God's way is Peace, Prosperity, Prayer, Praise, and Promotion.

- "May the peace of God which passes all understanding rest, rule and abide (live) with you now, hence forth, and even forevermore."

- "My peace I give unto you, not as the world giveth, give I unto you."

- "Beloved, I wish above all things, that thou mayest prosper and be in health even as thy soul prospers."

- "Men ought always to pray and never to cease." Prayer keeps us in a position of humbleness and humility unto God. It keeps us in contact with our Father, as his sons. We spend time with our Father and keep a right relationship in His kingdom.

Let's take a look at the differences between God's Kingdom and satan's kingdom:

God's Kingdom	Satan's kingdom
Peace	Pride (proud)
Prosperity (Through Prayer & Diligence)	Power (through domineering)
Praise (to God)	Praises from people
Promotion	Position through controlling Power
Humble	High-minded
Holy	Heady
Humility	Huge (In his own eyes)

God's word tells us to not think more highly of ourselves than we ought to.

Question: How could Satan enter Judas when he was one of the twelve disciples who walked continuously with Jesus every day for 3 ½ years?

Answer: The love of money was his area of weakness." As one of the disciples, he already had:

1. **Position – He was well known as a disciple.**

2. **People – he was always thronged with crowds of people; they looked at him as one of the disciples of Jesus.**

3. **Power – Jesus gave them power over all the unclean spirits, to cast them out. He was one of the twelve sent out two by two; however pride entered by betrayal: He was the only one of his disciples who lifted up his heel against Jesus. The Bible said that the serpent would bruise the heel of Jesus and Jesus would crush his head. But now why did Judas turn against Jesus. Face it; he already had the position, the people, and the authority (power). The answer is found in the fact that he loved and kept the purse or money. God said you cannot serve two masters; mammon (money) and God, for you will love the one and hate the other. He must have had a love of money.**

The Bible gives us an illustration of Judas' heart. There was a woman was caught up in a life of sin, and who desperately desired to be free. On the outside no one even suspected that she was truly tired of this type of life, but Jesus knew her heart, and one day spoke words of life, forgiveness, and encouragement to her. He had so impacted her life until she wanted to show her gratitude. One day a well known man named Simon invited Jesus to his house. And to everyone's amazement, who should appear without an invitation? You guessed it, this same woman.

She'd heard that Jesus was there, and forgetting all about not being invited, being a woman, and to boot a woman with a bad reputation, she made her way to the house. I'm sure she had to push her way through the doors, but no matter. Her heart was racing with so much excitement and joy until she totally disregarded the men's looks of contempt and disapproval. Upon seeing Jesus, she immediately knelt down crying. As her warm tears fell on his feet, she began wiping his feet with her hair and in complete brokenness and extreme gratitude, she kissed his feet.

She had come to pour upon him all the love she could. What do you give someone who has given you new life? She broke open an alabaster box full of precious ointment and poured it upon Jesus. What a precious, intimate scene. However, what did Judas see? He saw this ointment being wasted for it cost about one year's salary. To him it was wasted

because it was not sold and the money put into the moneybag or purse that he was holding for Jesus and his ministry.

Judas, as many today, was not looking at the good of others, but rather thinking about himself and his lustful greed of money. Imagine, it is the root of all evil, not just some of the evil, but A-L-L evil!!! He evaluated Jesus' worth in comparison to the money's worth. In other words, he put them both on a scale and in his mind, the money outweighed Jesus.

Ask God to examine your heart and reveal to you any hidden motives, agendas, and perhaps even pride that may be bothering you. The good thing about God is that he is very loving and is here to help us in our areas of weakness. Jesus is ever living to make intercession for us before the Father God. Go for it! You'll find that he is waiting to hear from you and to cleanse you from all unrighteousness. Judas never asked Jesus for help, he never confessed the thoughts going on in his mind. You today have an opportunity to talk with Jesus about what's going on inside of you, in your heart and mind. You have a choice to repent and allow Him to bring healing and fullness of joy.

Acknowledge that He is your all in all. He can't be compared with anyone or anything. God is everything! When you realize this and live your life this way, you'll discover an inner peace that money can never buy or replace. You'll love and serve one Master, the Almighty God and allow money to be your servant. It will serve you for the fulfillment of God's plans.

Since our total development depends upon our lives being balanced, it is important to keep track of each area. The following chart will help you by displaying a picture of where your growth is now and your periodic development over the next 12 months. Enter your current scores on a scale of 1-10, with 10 being the highest. This should give you a pretty good indication of where you are in your spirit, soul, and body. Continue to retake the test every 3 months.

As you record your scores, you will be amazed at the growth.

SPIRITUAL

	Now	3 Months	6 Months	12 Months
Prayer Life	_____	_____	_____	_____
Bible Study Time	_____	_____	_____	_____
Word Meditation/Reflection	_____	_____	_____	_____
Worship/Praise to God	_____	_____	_____	_____
Church Attendance	_____	_____	_____	_____
Tithing	_____	_____	_____	_____
Giving	_____	_____	_____	_____
TOTAL SCORE	_____	_____	_____	_____
(Possible 70 points)				

SOUL

	Now	3 Months	6 Months	12 Months
Friendships	_____	_____	_____	_____
Relationships	_____	_____	_____	_____
Work/Labor	_____	_____	_____	_____
Credit Conditions	_____	_____	_____	_____
Financial Increase	_____	_____	_____	_____
Debt Structure (Debts Paid)	_____	_____	_____	_____
Personal/Alone Time	_____	_____	_____	_____
Mind Expansion/Learning	_____	_____	_____	_____
Helping Others/Service	_____	_____	_____	_____
Goal Setting	_____	_____	_____	_____
Goal Accomplishments	_____	_____	_____	_____
Attitude	_____	_____	_____	_____
TOTAL SCORE	_____	_____	_____	_____
(Possible 120 points) 120 points)				

BODY

	Now	3 Months	6 Months	12 Months
Healthy Eating Habits	_____	_____	_____	_____
Physical Exercise (Regularly)	_____	_____	_____	_____
Vitamins/Minerals (Daily)	_____	_____	_____	_____
Routine Doctor Visits	_____	_____	_____	_____
Rest/Sleep	_____	_____	_____	_____
TOTAL SCORE	_____	_____	_____	_____
(Possible 50 points)				

SPIRIT/SOUL/BODY GRAPH CHART

Spiritual	Soul	Body
70	120	50
65	110	47
60	100	45
55	90	40
50	80	35
45	70	30
35	60	25
30	50	20
25	40	15
20	30	10
15	20	5
10	10	3
0	0	0

"Beloved, I wish above all things that thou mayest prosper and be in health, even as thy soul prospers." III John 1:2

How is your soul prospering? You will prosper to the extent that your soul prospers. Your soul is your mind, will, and emotions. Our lives should be balanced in all areas.

The above chart reflects your balance. Place a dot by the number above reflecting your total score in each area. Then draw a line from dot to dot (connecting the dots). This should give you a pretty good indication of your personal balance.

Set goals to work on any area that is out of balance.

(See Areas To Improve)

AREAS TO IMPROVE CHART

List steps you will take toward your goal of improvement.

SPIRITUAL REALM GROWTH

3 Months	6 Months	12 Months
_____	_____	_____
_____	_____	_____
_____	_____	_____
_____	_____	_____
_____	_____	_____

SOUL REALM GROWTH

3 Months	6 Months	12 Months
_____	_____	_____
_____	_____	_____
_____	_____	_____
_____	_____	_____
_____	_____	_____

BODY REALM GROWTH

3 Months	6 Months	12 Months
_____	_____	_____
_____	_____	_____
_____	_____	_____
_____	_____	_____
_____	_____	_____

TOTAL DEVELOPMENT WEEKLY CHART

You may score yourself weekly on the Balanced Life Chart. If you so desire, then list here any area where you scored under 10 on the Balanced Life Chart, list your goals to bring it up to 10. Utilize the following weekly checklist to chart your progress. (Remember that there are no perfect 10's in all areas.)

Area _____

Current Date: _____ Current Score: _____

  Date:_____ 1st Week Score:_____
  Date:_____ 2nd Week Score:_____
  Date:_____ 3rd Week Score:_____
  Date:_____ 4th Week Score:_____
  Date:_____ 5th Week Score:_____
  Date:_____ 6th Week Score:_____

Area _____

Current Date: _____ Current Score: _____

  Date:_____ 1st Week Score:_____
  Date:_____ 2nd Week Score:_____
  Date:_____ 3rd Week Score:_____
  Date:_____ 4th Week Score:_____
  Date:_____ 5th Week Score:_____
  Date:_____ 6th Week Score:_____

Area _____

Current Date: _____ Current Score: _____

  Date:_____ 1st Week Score:_____
  Date:_____ 2nd Week Score:_____
  Date:_____ 3rd Week Score:_____
  Date:_____ 4th Week Score:_____
  Date:_____ 5th Week Score:_____
  Date:_____ 6th Week Score:_____

Area _____

Current Date: _____ Current Score: _____

  Date:_____ 1st Week Score:_____
  Date:_____ 2nd Week Score:_____
  Date:_____ 3rd Week Score:_____
  Date:_____ 4th Week Score:_____
  Date:_____ 5th Week Score:_____
  Date:_____ 6th Week Score:_____

Area _____

Current Date: _____   Current Score: _____

    Date:_____   1st Week Score:_____
    Date:_____   2nd Week Score:_____
    Date:_____   3rd Week Score:_____
    Date:_____   4th Week Score:_____
    Date:_____   5th Week Score:_____
    Date:_____   6th Week Score:_____

Area _____

Current Date: _____   Current Score: _____

    Date:_____   1st Week Score:_____
    Date:_____   2nd Week Score:_____
    Date:_____   3rd Week Score:_____
    Date:_____   4th Week Score:_____
    Date:_____   5th Week Score:_____
    Date:_____   6th Week Score:_____

Area _____

Current Date: _____   Current Score: _____

    Date:_____   1st Week Score:_____
    Date:_____   2nd Week Score:_____
    Date:_____   3rd Week Score:_____
    Date:_____   4th Week Score:_____
    Date:_____   5th Week Score:_____
    Date:_____   6th Week Score:_____

Area _____

Current Date: _____   Current Score: _____

    Date:_____   1st Week Score:_____
    Date:_____   2nd Week Score:_____
    Date:_____   3rd Week Score:_____
    Date:_____   4th Week Score:_____
    Date:_____   5th Week Score:_____
    Date:_____   6th Week Score:_____